TABLE OF CONTENTS

Top 20 Test Taking Tips

1. Carefully follow all the test registration procedures
2. Know the test directions, duration, topics, question types, how many questions
3. Setup a flexible study schedule at least 3-4 weeks before test day
4. Study during the time of day you are most alert, relaxed, and stress free
5. Maximize your learning style; visual learner use visual study aids, auditory learner use auditory study aids
6. Focus on your weakest knowledge base
7. Find a study partner to review with and help clarify questions
8. Practice, practice, practice
9. Get a good night's sleep; don't try to cram the night before the test
10. Eat a well balanced meal
11. Know the exact physical location of the testing site; drive the route to the site prior to test day
12. Bring a set of ear plugs; the testing center could be noisy
13. Wear comfortable, loose fitting, layered clothing to the testing center; prepare for it to be either cold or hot during the test
14. Bring at least 2 current forms of ID to the testing center
15. Arrive to the test early; be prepared to wait and be patient
16. Eliminate the obviously wrong answer choices, then guess the first remaining choice
17. Pace yourself; don't rush, but keep working and move on if you get stuck
18. Maintain a positive attitude even if the test is going poorly
19. Keep your first answer unless you are positive it is wrong
20. Check your work, don't make a careless mistake

Developing, Communicating, and Sustaining an Educational Vision

Educational vision and goals

Stating values and ideals

Administrators need to stay true to what the school feels their values and ideals are because without a vision and focus, creating policies to move the school in a positive direction will be much more difficult to do. Having a clear mission about where the school should be going will help the instructional focus of teachers and in return help influence student learning. Administrators play the biggest role in developing the goals; however, they should not decide these alone, this should be as a group effort. Administrators need to get teachers, students and parents involved. Without a clear focus, the organizational culture will be harder to change in a positive direction. Administrators are extremely busy and can easily get caught up in the everyday duties of managing a school, however, it is important to try and stay on the path of what the mission of school is and not lose sight of it.

Community needs

When an administrator is trying to determine which educational needs are the most important to meet, it is important that he or she looks at the community needs. Some communities need to know that when they send their children to school they are going to be safe; others may need to know that their children are getting the best education possible. Different communities have different needs. Administrators need to get involved with the parents and find out what they expect from their child's

school. Ignoring the parent's expectations can have a negative effect on the administrator. The parents could start to complain and the leadership status of the administrator could suffer from it. It is also important to look at the population projections. These types of population projections can help give an indication of how fast the school is going to grow and which ethnicity groups are coming in. This is important because different ethnicity groups also have different needs.

Community of leaders

Effective administrators know the importance of building a community of leaders which includes staff members, parents and students. When others feel they are apart of a group, then they take responsibility for learning, commit to school goals and know why those goals are important. Many times when teachers, parents and students are told what to do they merely just go along with it and never get to take ownership in anything. This creates everyone to take a passive role rather than taking an active role in the education process. Effective administrators know that empowering others to take part in the school's mission can have a powerful impact on the student's achievement. Administrators must also provide the necessary resources and support in order to allow others to become community leaders.

School-community relations

It is extremely important for an administrator to maintain school-community relations because it helps to maintain the all around well being of the school. This is especially true if the school has diverse ethnic groups and values. Administrators need to make sure that every group is recognized and their values are considered important. If parents feel their values are important then they will be more likely to have an active part in their child's education. Administrators can also use community resources in the educational process. The resources could be donations for science projects, books or just parent volunteers. If there is a diverse range of cultures, then individuals could come and share their culture with others. Using community resources get everyone involved in education process.

Parental involvement. Parents are often hesitant about getting involved with the school functions because they often feel they are not important and their opinions do not count. In some cases parents may have had a negative experience involving a principal or other school functions, therefore, it is the responsibility of the administrator to make those parents feel valued and important not only to the school but to their child before discussing any type of involvement. An effective administrator knows the value of parental involvement and realizes they must invite, recruit and motivate all parents to get involved. Many times when these efforts do not work an administrator may have to offer incentives or rewards in order to get parents to take that first step toward involvement. Involving a parent does not mean they have to speak in public or put on a carnival, it could as simple as donating time to repair something in the school.

Community volunteers. Effective administrators know that in order to build a successful school culture, community volunteers need to play a vital role. Asking community members to volunteer their time will help boost their self esteem and make help them realize they can have a major impact on the student's learning. If there is a strong volunteer program then parents and community members can become actively involved in their child's education and feel their skills are useful and important. This bond will help break down the barriers between teachers and parents. Community volunteers can also have a major impact on the teacher's lives. If volunteers are actively helping to meet the student's needs, then this can give the teachers more time to plan other activities in the lesson plan. Their scheduling can become more flexible.

Soliciting support for vision and goals

Choice of staff
After the administrator has developed a clear vision and set goals for the school, it is now time to find individuals that can share in the same vision. An administrator must remember that every time a position must be filled, whoever fulfills that position could change the school culture. It would be impossible to find someone who shares the exact same vision as the person who just left that position. However, it is important that they at least have common goals and ideals and the administrator should strongly emphasize certain values and ideals during the hiring process. The administrator is the one who has to power to hire, promote and demote and it is important that similar values are shared because it could take years to rebuild an organizational culture again.

Formal leadership appointments
Another way an administrator can shape the organizational culture is making leadership appointments within the organization. Leadership appointments include positions such as a chairperson or department head. Before making these decisions, the administrators must carefully consider who best reflects and will promote the mission, goals and ideals of the school. This is a way of making an example of someone to the others in the school who he or she thinks possess important values and ideals. This could be a time when the administrator emphasizes why these individuals were chosen for the key positions and qualities

Copyright © Mometrix Media. You have been licensed one copy of this document for personal use only. Any other reproduction or redistribution is strictly prohibited. All rights reserved.

they possess that make them the best candidate for the position. However, an administrator must be prepared for the chance of conflict and resentment from others because they were not chosen. This could have a negative impact on the school environment.

Informal leaders
Administrators can have an influence on shaping the school culture by appointing leadership positions, however, there are informal leaders of the school and the administrator has no control over who that is. Informal leaders are individuals that others look up to and seek guidance from. Therefore, if an administrator wants to shape the organizational culture, then he or she needs to identify, become familiar with and develop a relationship with informal leaders. Many times the informal leaders are already in place before the administrator even takes the position at the school. If the administrator wants their goals achieved it will be crucial to develop a commitment from the leaders. There will be many times when the informal leader is the same person who is the formal leader. Many times this informal leader is the person who has the greatest interaction with others and their opinions and values are respected by many.

Initiating and managing change

Group meetings
Group meetings are a common occurrence in the educational field. In most cases the administrator will be the lead the group and be in charge of planning and conducting the meetings. However, there will be times when someone else will be responsible for carrying out those functions however; administrators are responsible to make sure the functions are carried out in an effective and productive way. Many times administrators believe their meetings are meaningful and productive, however,

many times staff members see them as a waste of time. Teachers often feel meetings do not provide resourceful information and the planning of them is unsatisfactory. Administrators must make sure the information given is valuable and meetings are planned for a purpose and not to just hand out papers.

Techniques for success. If an administrator can communicate in a certain manner, this can create a more encouraging environment. If an administrator can open a meeting by just stating their true feeling or their reaction to a certain situation, then this can create a more secure environment. Opening with these kinds of statements can put a staff at ease because they know there is a common ground that has just been developed. It is always crucial that an administrator talk to the staff in a non threatening manner; nothing will cause a person to become defensive faster than if they are under the assumption they are being attacked personally. An administrator must also learn how to become accepting of others and that includes their personality, opinions and approaches. Another important consideration is to remember that an administrator can control the attitude of the group. If he or she comes in and is positive about a situation, then the chances are the group will be more positive.

Challenging of authority
When an administrator is faced with a negative reaction to authority, their first reaction may be to become defensive or become upset. However, the appropriate way to handle this situation is to investigate and examine the reasons why others are responding this way. This may be a difficult reaction to have for many administrators. The feelings of hurt and anger are normal, however, an effective administrator knows how to put those feelings behind them and move on to the problem solving stage. The challenging of

authority can be a positive situation, especially if the causes are understood. The key to diagnosing the reasons for the negative reaction is to have a discussion with the parties involved. Every effort should be made to avoid putting anyone on the defensive and every attempt should be made to understand the person's point of view.

*Exercising authorityguidelines.*There are numerous reasons why people question and challenge authority. However, if an administrator follows certain guidelines, then this issue can be overcome. Administrators are obviously going to have to make some very difficult decisions and give directives to others. One consideration an administrator should decide on is how and in what style the directive will be given. It is important for an administrator to remember that regardless of how professional the directive was given, if the person who received it does not feel that it is in their best interest, there is going to be an issue of resistance. An administrator should also consider the strengths and weaknesses of the person before giving a directive. Issuing an order for someone who is not motivated will result in failure. They should also explain the rationale behind the directive and remember not everyone may understand the value in it.

Principles and processes of change

Awareness stage of innovation
The first stage an administrator will go through is the awareness stage which is becoming aware of a new innovation, but not having enough information about it. Many times an administrator may not even have a strong enough interest in finding out more information about the subject. At the interest stage, an administrator is beginning to show signs of interest and desire to gather more information and may even begin to develop negative or positive feelings. At the mental stage, the administrator has decide this is something worth trying and is evaluating the innovation and deciding how it will be implemented. They may also ask respected members of the school community to assess it. During the trial stage the innovation is implemented on a trial basis. Next is the adoption stage and this is the point when the innovation is implemented fully. The last stage is the integration stage and the new innovation is now a routine.

Unsuccessful innovations
Many times innovations are unsuccessful because teachers feel they do not understand what their responsibility is in their new role regardless if they had the orientation before the process began. Administrators should never assume that teachers will fully understand their roles after one or two orientation sessions. Receiving feedback is crucial in the beginning. Teachers may also feel they lack the knowledge and skills to fulfill their duties. Administrators must ensure teachers receive the proper training and assistance needed to fulfill their duties. Another reason innovations fail is due to the lack of materials the teachers need. If an administrator wants an innovation to succeed, it is their responsibility to make sure material is available in a sufficient quantity. Innovations are often unsuccessful because certain aspects of the school program were not changed to assist the teacher's new role.

Needs assessment
There will be times when an administrator is forced to face the pressure of making changes within the school. The first and most important stage in the process of change is using a needs assessment plan that provides important information about the strengths and weaknesses about the various educational programs and activities the school is currently using. If the administrator does not occasionally assess the current

educational program then most likely he or she will be unaware of any needed change and assume all programs are working well and meeting the needs of everyone. This assessment will also help others understand the need for change. Once there has been a decision to change the program, alternatives need to be selected. One alternative is to replace the current program or just modify it. The administrator should choose the alternative that will best help to improve the school.

Reducing resistance
There are certain groups who will be affected the most when there is change; the faculty, the students, the parents, the school board, the administrator's superiors and the state department of public instruction. These groups can also provide the most support or the most resistance to change. Administrators must remember every group will have their opinions, and the most professional thing to do is respect, listen and accept those opinions even if they are not agreed upon. One of the most important groups an administrator needs to consider during the change process is the faculty. It is crucial to get the faculty involved because if the faculty does not understand why there needs to be a change, there will be less support and in return an implementation of a new program might not be successful.

Teachers and change
Teachers will worry when there is going to be a change, however administrators can ease those fears by providing adequate information about why the change is being made. Administrators should still be sensitive about teacher's fears and ensure they are provided with reassurance. One of the first fears teachers will have is wondering how the change will affect them personally. If these fears can be eliminated then there may be concerns about whether or not

they will know how to perform the tasks that will be required of them. After those concerns have been eliminated, next will come questions about how the new change will affect the students. The best thing for an administrator to do is to listen and ensure the staff that their concerns are important and being heard.

Power struggle bargaining
An administrator can possibly find themselves in a situation where they feel strongly about their objectives and conflict cannot be avoided, and chances are an agreement is impossible. This situation is called power struggle bargaining. The administrator will do everything it takes to resolve this conflict; however they may be convinced the solution must go their way. This can cause hurt feelings and destroy many personal and professional relationships with individuals that may be involved with this situation. Many times conflict may seem to be resolved, however it will reappear in future situations. However, the advantage to power struggle bargaining is that the conflict may end in complete favor of the administrator. It may be necessary for an administrator to get involved in this power struggle; however, if they want the conflict to end in their favor they must assess their power and authority accurately or there could be disastrous results.

Conflict initiation strategy
In most cases, administrators will want to prevent conflict from happening and may find it impossible to prevent conflict. However, if an administrator finds themselves in a situation where an individual or group is not performing at the level they should and does not want to change; it may be cause for the administrator to actually initiate conflict. If an administrator is in a situation where he or she observes a problem with a teacher and the teacher disagrees, the avoidance of conflict will not be possible.

It is the administrator's responsibility to ensure that all staff members are performing to the best of their abilities, and conflict may be needed in order to bring about improvement. It is important that all possible outcomes are considered before conflict is initiated and that conflict is absolutely necessary for improvement.

Using data sources

Researchbased programs
It is important for administrators not to rush and implement programs that do not have solid research and results. Many times new programs can just add more activities to the curriculum and not fit the needs of the students or they can conflict with what the school's mission is. Many research articles and journals can say that a certain program can bridge the learning gap however; it may not work in every school. Administrators need to stay focus and remember what works best for their school and stay on that course. An effective administrator should only use programs that can produce solid research-based results. It is always important for an administrator to know what the needs are for their students and school before making any huge program change.

Evaluation of student performance
Effective administrators know that in order to keep the school progressing, there needs to be a monitoring system of tests, feedback and evaluating student performance. The data collected from standardized tests and state assessments is important but they do not give a complete picture of the student's progression. These tests are resourceful to the teacher in order to plan for daily instruction. The more relevant feedback comes from monthly curriculum-based assessments. These help keep teachers and administrators focused on specific goals that are more short-term and easily measurable. Without collecting the data from these sources, teachers and administrators will have a more difficult knowing if the instruction and curriculum is meeting the needs of the students. They are left to guess about their success. However, if a school does collect all the important data, it needs to be organized in an orderly fashion.

Collaborative decision making

Stakeholder identification
In order to involve stakeholders in the decision making process, an administrator must first identify them. Stakeholders in education can be any group involved with education; however, the most notable groups are students, faculty members, teachers, administration, parents, school board members, legislators and community leaders. All these groups have a powerful impact on education. Many stakeholders want to take an active part in education while others choose to take a more passive role. Allowing stakeholders, especially parents, to be a part of the decision making process can have a positive impact on their child's educational achievements and emotional development. Their ideas and opinions can be extremely helpful and it creates a unity between parents, teachers and administrators. However, there can be drawbacks, for example, if one group of stakeholders takes an active part, they can have too much power. There is a chance that this power could be used to create conflict.

Teamwork
A school-based community involves everyone in the decision making process including teachers, parents and students. Each team is responsible for a certain part that will improve the school and with all three teams working together it will promote a school-based community that focuses on trying to continue to improve

the school. This type of community will help student behavior, performance and will encourage parents to take an active part in their child's education. When the teams are able to work together and make decisions it creates a feeling of ownership and responsibility. Everyone is aware of the school's goals and will know what direction they want to take the school. It may be difficult at times for everyone to agree on certain issues, however, the conflict may be reduced if individuals can agree on issues by using a "no fault" problem solving, collaboration and making decisions by consensus. These methods work better than voting because with voting there is an increased chance of individuals taking sides.

Educational problem solving

Effective communication
Administrators can be effective communicators by attending to others. This does not mean an administrator must to show up at all the school functions, PTA meetings, concerts and other functions, this means to be helpful and attentive. Many times administrators are so busy that while engaging in a conversation with a teacher, parent or student they are really are trying to complete other things and not fully listening to the conversation. This can give the other person the implication they are not important or they are a nuisance. Effective administrators know the importance of using the eyes, body and face to give another person their undivided attention. This makes a clear statement to the other person that the administrator is listening fully to what they have to say. When holding a meeting it is important that the administrator is free from distractions. This may mean they may have to turn of their cell phone, pagers or palm pilots.

Confronting and solving stakeholder issues
Every administrator should know how to effectively help solve problems with staff, students and parents. It is important for each administrator to be prepared to confront issues, explore them and then know how to consider possible solutions. When a staff member, student or parent approaches an administrator with a problem, the administrator should react in the appropriate manner. It is important that the administrator listen attentively with an open mind and also empathize with that person. They need to make that staff member, student or parent feel as though their problem matters and they feel important. After they have truly listened and understood the issues it is time to gain more information about the issue. The administrator should ask questions about the content of the issue and the person's feelings. The last step is to set goals and problem solving steps in order to resolve the issue.

Asking questions. In order for an administrator to gather information on a certain issue, it is important that an administrator ask the right questions. This is a way for him or her to investigate the true matter of the situation. However, the administrator does not want to ask so many questions because it may appear that the other person in the conversation is being interrogated. Questions should only be asked in a way that will extend the conversation and the administrator can gather more information that is more difficult to get in other ways. Open-ended questions are acceptable when they are asked in brief conversations and in a more public environment or if there are times when asking questions is in a threatening or dangerous situation.

Effectiveness feedback
If an administrator wants to hear truly informative feedback about their messages and job performance they must

expand their sources. Many times their sources are limited because there is a misconception about the administrator's receptivity to only positive communication. Staff and other members of the school community may feel their opinions and ideas will only cause them trouble and do not express their opinions honestly especially ones who have disagreeable views. This could lead to a situation where the administrator only receives feedback and evaluations from a group of people who view things in the same or similar way as the administrator. It is crucial that an administrator receive feedback from a variety of sources in order to do their job effectively and to serve everyone's best interest.

Role expectations

Administrator behavior

The behavior of an administrator can be influenced by different factors including the role expectations of others and personal need dispositions. There will less conflict if the administrator's personal needs and the expectations of others are similar in nature, when they clash there is a likelihood conflict will occur. It is not a necessity that the administrator conform to other's expectations, however, it is important that the administrator at least understands them. There will be several different groups, including teachers, parents, students, school board members and community leaders that will expect the administrator to act in a certain way in a situation. It would be impossible for an administrator to understand why all of these groups have these expectations; therefore, the administrator should focus more time on developing relationships that could have a positive impact on their effectiveness.

Direction of expectations. An administrator could experience the direction of expectations from the group

having total agreement or they could completely oppose something. The main factor in determining the direction of the group depends on the situation and the decision making process. That is why it is so crucial for an administrator to understand the group's role expectations. A situation may occur when one group is accepting of the administrator making a decision without consulting them; however, the opposite may be true in another situation. It is important that an administrator carefully evaluate the situation and then base the decision making process on what he or she understands about the group's expectations. Conflict will sure to arise if the situation is handled in an opposing manner than what the group expects.

Importance of clarity

Role expectations are generally not written down in a manual or expressed directly to the administrator and many times the administrator may be completely oblivious of any role expectations from different groups. Another problem that may arise is different administrators may have a different understanding of certain terminology. If role expectations would be clearly communicated or possibly written this would help lessen the possibility of role uncertainty. Another factor that could cause conflict is the fact that many administrators have inaccurate perceptions. The possibility of role conflict can occur if expectations of the group and administrator were the same; however, the administrator believes they are different. Other situations that can cause conflict are the administrator believes the expectations are the same with the group, when in reality they are different or the administrator did not realize the group's strong belief in role expectations.

Intensity of role expectations

A group's expectations may be so intense that they believe there is only one way an administrator should act in a certain situation. An effective administrator must investigate and try to fully understand why the group feels so intense about certain situations. An administrator must be able to distinguish the difference between a group feeling as though there is only one way an administrator should act compared to maybe there are other ways of acting. If an administrator feels the situation causes the group to feel that "perhaps" he or she should respond a certain way, the administrator will feel much less pressure. This response would be completely different if the administrator felt it was essential to act a certain way. If administrators choose to ignore other's expectations in an intense situation, there is a chance they will complain and the administrator's status will suffer.

Intra-role conflict

Role expectations can also vary to the degree in which they are compatible, the expectations are at odds. In most cases role conflict is caused by incompatible expectations, however, if there is a lack of agreement in role expectations it may also increase the chance for conflict. Intra-role conflict is caused when the administrator is uncertain about themselves in regards to which role to play. This often occurs when a situation arises and the administrator is unsure about his or her role is and which role is the best to choose. This can be a difficult situation because the administrator is unable to be certain about what is best for the school. The best situation to be in is when there is conflict and the administrator is uncertain about which role to choose, however, they are certain of the correct action that should be taken.

Extra-role conflict

Extra-role conflict is a situation when certain groups want to challenge the role the administrator has chosen by imposing their own expectations. An administrator may require certain procedures to be done from all teachers regardless of their years of experience; in return teachers refuse to follow those procedures. Administrators are certain of the role they must play and are confident in their decision even though teachers are in complete disagreement. An administrator may be completely aware of the disagreement but they do not doubt which role is best. If the conflict is brought on the administrator because of external factors and not from inner doubts, it is referred to as extra-role conflict. This can be an extremely difficult situation for the administrator and it is important that it is handled in a professional manner.

Analyzing contributing factors for conflict

It is the responsibility of an administrator to work with a variety of individuals and groups, and everyone comes with different views, ideas and backgrounds. With this much interaction there is a strong likelihood that there will be conflict about which role is appropriate for the administrator to play. Many times an administrator's personality is incompatible with the roles that are expected. A person's personality cannot be changed. There could also be an incompatibility of what the administrator expects of themselves compared to what the group expects and an incompatibility of two or more group's expectations for the administrator's role. In many cases the same group does not agree what the expectations are. In this type of field it will be near impossible to have role conflict, however, effective administrators know how to handle it professionally.

There are effective steps an administrator can take in order to prevent role conflict, however, it is important that he or she realizes that their own personality, attitude and behavior could be the root of the problem. Administrators need to be aware of the fact that the way they treat people, make decisions and use their authority can cause conflict. Administrators should decide if conflict occurs because of unavoidable circumstances or if it could have been avoidable if the administrator had taken a different approach in certain situations. In most cases, the administrator may believe that other factors are the cause of conflict and not themselves, however, if an administrator wants to be effective, then he or she must at least consider the possibility that the problem may be them.

Consequences of role conflict

There is a wide variety of consequences of role conflict. If an administrator is constantly finding themselves in situations where they are in conflict it can very frustrating and cause stress and tension. It could possibly impair their effective decision making or the worst consequence is being dismissed from their position. In regards to the individual whose group is always at conflict with the administrator, it could cause them to have a negative attitude toward others, especially the administrator. These continual negative feelings can create a hostile attitude toward the administrator and in return create a lack of interest in the school and the goals. This would only have a negative impact on the students who are in that teacher's class. The impact that is felt by individuals in regards to conflict can be major or minor. Conflict cannot be avoided; however, the determining factor on how major the impact will be is based on how well the conflict is handled.

Dealing with conflict

Administrators can choose from four different options about how to deal with conflict:

1. One option is to use the *cooperative approach* which means to hear other's points of view and show empathy toward that group's feelings. After this has been accomplished then the administrator can attempt to find a compromise that will lead toward a mutual solution.
2. Another approach is *confirming*, which means the administrator communicates to the groups that he or she feels they have a great deal of competency and they are highly respected for it.
3. Another option is to use the *competitive approach*, which views conflict as a win-lose battle. One of the groups at conflict must back down from the conflict and it is only then that the conflict will end.
4. The last option an administrator has is to use the *avoidance approach*. This approach is when the groups stop discussing the situation and end the conflict but do not resolve any issues.

Approach effectiveness. Research has shown that administrators who use both the cooperative and confirming approaches have much more success in resolving conflict. Those who choose to use the competitive or avoidance approaches are less likely to succeed in conflict resolution. The cooperative and confirming approaches are considered to be more successful because when an individual feels they are recognized for their competence they feel a sense of security and value and more likely to want to resolve the conflict. The competitive approach seems to be less effective because many times the administrator will use this approach when he or she thinks they can win the conflict and they use the avoidance approach when they are uncertain of how to handle the situation. The cooperative and confirming approaches requires the administrator to have strong interpersonal skills and if they are lacking these special skills, then it is best for the administrator to designate someone who does possess these skills.

Conflict resolution techniques

Conflict avoidance methods

Other techniques that can be used for conflict resolution are techniques called conflict avoidance methods.

- One of these techniques is called the *withdrawal method* in which an administrator will not argue in a certain situation and just accept the outcome.
- Another method is *indifference*, this is when an administrator makes it seem as though an issue does not matter to them personally.
- An administrator can also avoid any circumstances that would cause conflict, this method is called *isolation*.
- Using the *smooth over method* would mean the administrator accepts the situation and minimizes any arguments.
- The *consensus method* allows others to discuss their views and try to persuade others.

Although these methods avoid conflict they do not resolve it. These methods may be necessary to use, especially in situations when one group feels powerless in changing the views of the other group.

Problem-solving approach

The problem-solving approach is another method of conflict resolution and can be the most effective. However, this method is most likely to be successful if the parties are willing to compromise and an agreement is possible. It is also important that both parties can contribute something valuable and they are reassured and confident that the solution will made that will not exclude their interests. Each group should be allowed the opportunity to state their opinions and their conflicting positions. The group members should also state the opinions and position of the opponents as way of assuring their opponents that their points of view were heard and understood. This way the administrator can also ensure each group is clearly listening to the other. An administrator should then clarify with the groups if there is still conflict. Group members should state why their opinions and views are valid to them. When all members are through stating their viewpoints, the members should be asked if they have anything that needs to be added. There is a possibility that conflict may still be unavoidable.

Fact finding and misinterpretations. Once the administrator has heard each party's point of view about the dispute, it is important for the administrator to then validate the facts of the situation. Many times individuals will consider their opinions to be the facts and the absolute truth; however those facts need to be verified. It is very common that a person's emotions can distort their memory and the true facts of the situation. The administrator must also recognize that individuals in the conflict can agree on the facts; however their interpretations are complete opposite. The administrator's goal while in the process of fact finding is to clarify the areas that the parties do agree upon and narrow down the issues that are at disagreement. The administrator is put in the position to act as mediator; this role will be much easier to play if he or she is not one of the parties at conflict. If they are, then it is best if a neutral person acts as mediator.

Arbitration

There will be many times when conflict cannot be resolved using mediation; it may be necessary to use arbitration. This process involves the parties at conflict explaining their point of view to a third party who is the arbitrator. Each party must agree to accept the third party's decision and they must commit to carry out the arbitrator's decision when they agree to discuss the issue with the arbitrator. The best way to choose the person to be the arbitrator is to base the decision on the type of conflict and the circumstances surrounding it. Using an outside party for arbitration is not common; it is more common to use a superior in the organization. The growing trend of arbitration is a reflection on the fact that traditional means of conflict resolution is failing to achieve results.

Diversity—Leadership strategies

Diverse populations

Administrators need to look at what the population is regarding their school. If there is a diverse population then there could be diverse educational needs as well. In a diverse population there are people of all races and ethnicity groups and each race and ethnicity group has different expectations. It is so important that an administrator recognizes this and ensures that the groups know they are important and their voices will be heard. Another population group that should be recognized is the mobile population. If a school services a mobile population group, for example, a homeless shelter, it is important to recognize their needs may not have anything to do with education. Their needs may be just to keep their children fed. Another important factor in determining educational needs is gender.

Boys and girls are different emotionally, mentally and physically and their educational needs are different too.

Special education services

In order for a student to receive special education services, they must first be evaluated and if the individual who interprets the evaluation information decides special education services are needed then the student will have access to them. It must be decided which services are needed in order to meet the student's needs and a team of individuals will decide what the action plan will be. This plan is called the Individualized Education Program. This is a law binding agreement and an Administrator must ensure all individuals are following this plan and the student is receiving the services needed to have student achievement. A student may require more than one service in order to benefit from special education; these services can include speech therapy, counseling services, physical therapy, transportation or audiology services.

Gifted and talented programs

Each school has a gifted and talented program and one of the duties of an administrator is to oversee the organizational and operational feature of the program. Administrators need to ensure the policies written for the school are carried out and performed appropriately. If a student is performing at a higher level or has the potential to perform at a higher level, then those students selected should participate in an ongoing screening procedure. Administrators need to ensure that the assessment collected for the student is from multiple sources. It is important that all students from different populations and backgrounds have been given a consideration for the program. A committee that has been well trained in the area of gifted students will make the final selection. Administrators must also ensure of the proper appeals of district decisions especially those requested by parents.

Managing Change, Making Decisions, and Ensuring Accountability

Theories of leadership

Path-goal theory

This theory describes the type of leadership that was created so that leaders could encourage and support their team members to achieve goals that have already been set by providing a path they could follow. Leaders can make the path easier to travel by eliminating any factors that may cause the followers to be unsuccessful and provide awards while they are following the path. Removing any roadblocks will help team members feel capable of achieving the goal and providing awards will help them feel encouraged. The disadvantage with this theory is that it assumes there is only one way of achieving goals and that the leader is the only one who can create a correct path. It does not allow for others to develop their own ideas and creative ways of achieving goals.

Transformational leadership

Transformational leadership is the type of leadership that is created through individuals and not over them. This type of leadership requires group decision making, empowering teachers and knowing the value and process of change. An individual who can demonstrate transformational leadership knows how to create a team-like atmosphere and is always focusing on school improvement. An individual with this type of leadership qualities knows the importance of implementing the team approach and knows this is difficult because there is a reassignment of roles. When everyone is working as a team, everyone contributes and feels a sense of ownership within the school community. Teachers will want to perform at a higher level and in return student achievement will be higher. The administrator will have created a unified school community.

Situational leadership

Situational leadership is based more on the situation and not the person. Different situations call for a different style of leadership. This theory states that an administrator should base their style of leadership based on the situation they are facing. In some cases an individual may be chosen to lead in one situation and not chosen for another situation. Many times school boards may be looking for a person who can handle introducing change and at the same time be looking for someone who can be a mediator during conflict. This can cause a problem because as circumstances change the administrator who was chosen may not be needed now that the situation does not occur anymore. An administrator who is capable of situational leadership must be able to adapt and be flexible.

Decision making

Decision Process

Making a decision is a process that takes valued information and opinions from others and in return make a choice that you think is best. This whole process follows steps in order to achieve that decision:

1. The first step is *defining the situation* that needs a decision. This is the time to fully investigate and gain an understanding of what the problem is.
2. The next step is *identifying the alternatives* that can be used to make a decision. It is important for the administrator to know there can be more than two alternatives.

3. After identifying the alternatives, the next step is to *assess* them.
4. Then they should *consider* if they have the *resources* or power to implement a certain alternative and what kind of reception will they receive.
5. When a desirable alternative has been chosen, then it is time to *implement* it. An administrator may encounter resistance or complete acceptance.
6. After it has been implemented, the administrator should *evaluate* the decision and see if any other decisions need to be made.

Variety of Perspectives

In order for an administrator to be effective they must know the value of having a variety and diversified group of individuals in the school community. It is an advantage having individuals with a variety of perspectives on different situations because it can be valuable in the decision making and problem solving processes. It can be difficult for someone who has a preferred way of thinking to change and view a situation in another way. However, listening and understanding to other's points of views can make an administrator see that only one point view is not always the correct one to choose. The quality of a decision or implementation process can be greatly improved if there is a combination of different points of view.

Assessing effectiveness

Assessing decision making effectiveness is an important process in order for an administrator to improve as a decision maker. Administrators are extremely busy people and this can be a challenge to complete, therefore, often times this step is overlooked. It can be difficult for an administrator to be objective about their decision, especially since they have invested so much of their time. It might be helpful to involve outsiders who do not have vested interest in the assessment process. There is a chance that the decision's effectiveness could reflect negatively on the administrator. However, if the administrator wants continued improvement for their school, they should occasionally asses the effectiveness of their decision. Many times there will not be enough time to assess every time a decision is made; however, if he or she wants to improve their decision making skills, a periodic check will be in their best interest.

Decision making models

Rational model
The rational model for decision making is viewed as a process that first begins with the administrator admitting they are facing a problem. Then the administrator addresses this issue through a series of steps which in return comes out with an effective decision. This model focuses on what should be done and requires the administrator to follow certain actions that have already been designed to help achieve the best solution. It is assumed that the administrator is a rational administrator that works in an environment that functions rigidly and in a bureaucratic nature. Obviously, many school administrators do not work in this type of environment. This model does have some advantages; it clearly states the actions an administrator should take in certain situations and forces the administrator to decide which actions are most appropriate. However, this model has also shown that administrators are too quick in making decisions and do not attempt to try and find the true cause of the conflict.

Shared decision making
Shared decision making, which is also known as participatory or site-based decision making is also built on the idea of choice. This model states that choices are made by the administrator in order to

satisfy constraints. The focus of this model is on consensual decision making that is based on the values of the members in the group. The members of the decision making process also have open communication and everyone's status is equal. The whole idea of a participatory decision making theory centers on the idea of the way administrators make decisions versus how they should make decisions. Some critics believe this way of making decisions limits the control of the decision maker and they believe administrators are influenced by other's personalities and values more than their own reason or intelligence.

Situational model
This decision making model does not follow the traditional way of thinking. The administrator needs to take into consideration a variety of points and each point will affect the decision choice in some way. Certain situational variables can have an impact on how the administrator will make their decision choice. This model recognizes that administrators may need to take a different approach in deciding what is best for the school. A decision can be made regarding the goals of the school itself or just about the whole process. Other factors that administrators should take into consideration are ethical considerations, values, culture and climate. It is important that administrators are prepared that different situations will arise and the need for a decision may be needed immediately. The process will not be the same each time, different situations call for different decision making processes.
Strategic decision making
When an administrator uses this model, they are making a decision based on information they have gathered for their own knowledge and evaluating the internal and external environment. The environment is made up of interest

groups, negotiation, and informal power. In order for this model to work, the members need to identify what the obstacles are as well as what challenges may impact the decision choice. An administrator will want to use this model if they are interested in making a plan that has room for change, is flexible and has a long term effect. It is important that the individuals involved with this decision have the same philosophy and purpose in common. There will situations when unexpected events occur and an administrator may find themselves making decisions based on these unexpected events despite trying to strictly use the strategic decision making model.

Methods for promoting personal growth

Self-nurture
Administrators have an extremely difficult job; they must motivate, coach, lead, attend meetings and maintain the mission and goals of the school. These job duties can feel rewarding, however, they can also be emotionally draining. Many times this can cause burn out among many administrators and in return have a negative impact on the rest of the school. In order for an administrator to perform their responsibilities effectively they must remember they are individuals too, and need to take care of themselves. It is important for administrators to find a healthy balance between a work and personal life. Sleep, relaxation, fitness and a healthy diet will enable an administrator to be a well-adjusted person. When an administrator has found a way to balance their responsibilities, they become a healthier individual and in return a wonderful role model for staff members, students and parents.

Ethics and legal requirements

National Expectations

It is vital that administrators are aware of the national perspective concerning education. They need to know what is expected of them, their staff and their school. Administrators should know what the expectations are and make sure they are trying everything to meet those standards. The nation has certain goals that they expect schools to achieve and administrators need to know what is expected of them and ensure their school is moving in that direction. When an administrator knows what the national expectation is, they can look at their school and ask whether or not they have the means to achieve those expectations. If they do not then they will know what their educational needs are and find the means they need to achieve those goals.

Civil rights

It is crucial an administrator ensures the entire school is aware of other's civil rights. A person's civil rights are protections and privileges of personal power that is given to everyone by law. These rights are written in the Constitution and include the right to privacy, the right to a fair investigation, the right to vote and the right of equal protection. One of the most famous cases regarding civil rights is Brown v. Board of Education which involved the constitutionality of laws that enforced segregation in the educational system. In order to have an effective schools, it is vital that everyone and this includes, staff, students and parents respects and honors everyone's civil rights. This would enhance the sense of community and in return help with student achievement.

Due process

In the United States law, due process of law is a principle that states the government has a duty to respect all of a person's legal rights. The government cannot pick and choose which rights will be honored and which ones will not. Many states have their own guarantees of due process that are stated in their constitution. When a person must face a procedural due process, that individual has the right to be notified of any charges or proceedings that will involve him. Administrators must ensure that all staff member's right has been honored before any termination takes place. If a staff member feels that their rights have been violated and can prove it, there could be a cause for a law suit.

A special education due process hearing is when the parties present evidence to a qualified Hearing Officer who acts as the judge and jury. The Hearing Officer is not there to take sides, but rather listen to the evidence presented from both sides and write a Final Decision. There are certain laws that control the due process hearings, including the Individuals with Disabilities Education Improvement Act of 2004 and the federal regulations at 34 Code of Federal Regulations Part 300. It usually takes about 5 business days between the times the hearing was requested until the time when the Hearing Officer will contact the parties about a final decision. There is a 30 day timeframe that the parties must seek a resolution using methods such as the resolution process or mediation. There can be an extension granted if it is agreed upon by the Hearing Officer. Agreements can be made without the use of a Hearing Officer.

FERPA

The Family Educational Rights and Privacy Act (FERPA) is a Federal law that helps protect the privacy of student education records. Any school that receives funds from an applicable program of the U.S. Department of Education must obey this law. This law also gives the parents the right to examine their child's education held by the school. If a parent feels the record is incorrect they can make a request to change it, and if the school declines then the issue will go before a hearing. In most cases schools must have written consent before any information about the student is released. However, under FERPA the school can disclose to school officials who have a legitimate educational interest, to another school where the student is transferring, to financial aid agencies or to officials if there is a case of health and safety.

FOIA

The Freedom of Information Act (FOIA) was enacted in 1966 and states that any person has the right to request access to information or federal agency records. These agencies are required to disclose the information when the written request has been received; however there are nine exemptions that protect certain records from disclosure. If someone wants to make a request they must send an email, fax or mail a request to the U.S. Department of Education. There will be a response in 20 working days; however releasing records could take longer. In most states and local jurisdictions, they have their own laws about access to state and local records. Administrators must inform their staff about the privacy of school records. There should not be any information given out about a student unless it is to the student's parents or legal guardian.

IDEA

The Individuals with Disabilities Education Act (IDEA) was created to ensure that children with special needs are provided with a free appropriate public education and the services they need in order to meet their educational needs. It is the responsibility of the state and other public agencies to ensure the schools are giving the children with special needs the education and services they are entitled to at no cost to the parents and that they receive and

Individualized Education Program (IEP). The IEP is a document that states what the student needs in order to be successful in school. If there is a disagreement with the IEP the parent can ask for a due process hearing. A neutral hearing officer will make an independent decision that will possibly resolve the issue.

IEP

An Individualized Education Program (IEP) is a law binding individualized document that states what the plan is for a student with disabilities. Administrators must ensure the staff is abiding by this document at all times. These documents are created to give teachers, parents and related services personnel a chance to work as a team to ensure a student with disabilities is given an equal opportunity to succeed in school. In order to create an effective IEP the teachers, parents and other school staff must come together and discuss what issues the student has been facing. The student will then be evaluated and the eligibility will be decided. If the student is found eligible, then the appropriate services needed for the student will be decided. An IEP meeting is scheduled and in this meeting the findings from the evaluation will be discussed as well as what is needed to help the student. The IEP is then written with agreement of all parties, and the services will provided as well as a monitoring process.

It is required by law that certain information is included in the IEP. One piece of information that is required is at what level the student is performing on. This information is provided by evaluating assignments, tests, and observations by parents and teachers. Also required in the IEP are attainable goals the student can accomplish in a year. Many times these are not academic; they could pertain to social or physical aspects. It is important that all services

- 22 -

that are required are written into the document this also includes any modifications to the program. It must also contain information about the extent (if any) participation in a regular classroom and if they will participate in any state or district wide tests. Other information that is important includes dates and places of services, transition services needed, and measuring progress.

It is required by law that certain individuals play a role in writing a student's Individualized Education Program. If a person is qualified he or she may fill more than one of the team positions. The goal is to work as a team to write the IEP and a meeting to write it must be held within 30 calendar days from the day it was decided the student is eligible for special education and other services. The key members of this process are the parents because they know their child best and can contribute what strengths and weaknesses their child has. Other crucial participants are the teachers. There must be at least one regular teacher participating in the IEP meetings. The special education teacher provides important information about the appropriate ways to educate a student with special needs. Other important members are individuals that can interpret the student's evaluation, a school system representative, and an individual with expertise about the student.

Sex discrimination
Sex discrimination can affect employees, parents and students, therefore it is important that administrators are familiar with Title IX and ensure the school is following the guidelines of that policy. Title IX covers basically all public school districts because they receive federal financial assistance. If a school does not receive federal assistance, then Title IX does not apply to them. This policy covers programs that consist of

academic, extracurricular and athletics programs. It also covers all participants including parents, students and employees. Administrators must also ensure that everyone involved with the school including staff, parents and students are aware of the consequences of sexual harassment. It should be made clear that severe action will be taken if anyone is guilty of sexual harassment.

Communication and collaboration

Nonverbal skills
One of the most important skills in life is knowing how to communicate with others. This is extremely important especially when it comes to administrator leadership. Administrators are communicating with others all time even if they do not know it. Many of these communicating skills are non verbal. One way an administrator can communicate nonverbally is the way they dress. It is extremely important that the dress attire is appropriate and professional. The way an administrator stands is also a nonverbal communication. A person needs to be aware of their stance and realize that a certain position could communicate something negatively to another person even though that may not be the intention. Communication also involves listening and not just speaking. Effective administrators know that listening is not just about hearing the words coming from someone else's mouth it is about looking in the eyes of another and taking a serious interest into what they are saying.

Writing and speaking skills
Communicating with others is a vital part of anyone's life, especially an administrator. It is critical that administrators have appropriate writing and speaking skills in order to communicate effectively. In regards to writing skills, the content that has been written should be checked for spelling

and grammatical errors. A document with several misspelled words and grammatical errors does not appear to be professional. It is also important to remember that in this day and age of email, anything sent electronically can be misinterpreted. An administrator needs to be aware of proper etiquette concerning electronic communication. The recipient is unable to read a facial expression and many people consider something that is written in all caps as yelling. Speaking skills is another verbal skill that an administrator should know how to do effectively. It is important to use the proper tone and grammar. Words should be spoken with clarity and with confidence.

Message content
Many times when an administrator is communicating with others it is in a casual manner. However, there will be times when a more formal approach to communicating is needed. When this situation comes up, it is important that the words are constructed in a careful and thoughtful way. Before writing a message, the administrator needs to remember who the audience is, what the purpose of this message is and if this is going to be an oral or written form of communication. It is also important to remember that every word has the chance to be heavily scrutinized and weighed. When constructing their message, they need to make sure their idea is clear and the words chosen express the desired goal. If the goal is to persuade it is important to remember to acknowledge other opinions and remember that facts alone will not change an opinion.

Choosing communication channels
If an administrator wants to have an effective message then the communication channel chosen must be appropriate. The appropriate communication channel chosen should be based on the content of the message. An administrator needs to consider greatly what they are trying to say and decide whether or not the content of the message would be understood if it was presented in one form rather than another. The administrator needs to also factor in who the audience is; is it the students, parents or teachers. They also need to consider the size of the audience. Another factor to consider is the objectives of the message. It is also crucial for the administrator to be honest with themselves and recognize what their strengths and weaknesses are as a communicator. Certain communication channels may be more effective than others depending on their strengths.

Cross-cultural communication
An administrator should always take into account the different communication styles of the staff, parents and students. Everyone has learned how to communicate differently depending on who taught them, where they were raised and what culture they come from. It might take a little extra effort to become successful in communicating with someone from a different culture. There are a few differences to consider, one is frequency of eye contact. Some cultures discourage it. An administrator should always keep in mind the physical distance between the people they are communicating with, he or she does not want to invade a person's personal space. Another important factor to consider is speed of speech, it will be more difficult for someone to understand English if it is not their first language. It is also important to remember that listening is just as important as speaking.

Feedback
An administrator can send out a clear message that contains excellent grammar and a perfected tone; however that does not mean it was effective. The administrator's message will be effective if it was clearly understood and acted

upon as the administrator had intended it to be. An administrator must have enough courage to accept and receive feedback on the reactions to the message by the people who received it. Without feedback, an administrator will never know the true impact of their messages and may not make the necessary changes. Administrators should encourage true feedback and be able to take it gracefully if there are negative comments. Staff members should feel that their opinions matter and not live in fear that if they do express them; their jobs may be in jeopardy.

Effective public speaking
Effective public speaking skills are crucial to any administrator. They will be responsible to speak at many public events, PTA meetings, student assemblies or the school board. When speaking to the public, it is vital that an administrator speak louder than usual and use larger gestures than what he or she usually does. The attention of crowd will be lost if no one can hear the message. It is also important that the information given is up to date and written in an outline in order to stay on track. However, if notes are used, they should never be read from, they should only be used as a guide. It is wise to avoid the words, "um" and "ah," instead, just take a pause because these words are not professional to use. One way to help with public speaking is to videotape the speech a few days before, and then the administrator will know if any corrections need to be made.

Listening
An effective administrator must have strong speaking and writing skills, however, they must also know how to listen effectively. If an administrator does not know how to listen, he or she can misunderstand what is being communicated and this creates the possibility of more problems arousing. Listening involves more than hearing

words, it involves showing a genuine interest in what is said and a genuine empathy. Many people are not good listeners; this is a skill that takes practice and may even involve a change in attitude. There must be true interest in learning from others and hearing what another person has to say. An administrator may have to recognize that there needs to be a change in bad habits and developing good ones. Administrators can find many resourceful books written about listening effectively.

Communication barriers

Receiver barriers
Every message an administrator sends out will be interpreted in different ways from every person who receives it. Many times the message will not be successfully communicated simply because of factors that are not in the control of the administrator. Many times an administrator will send out a message they believe is extremely important and the persons receiving it do not share that same opinion. Many times the person receiving it may have a lack of interest of what is being said. Another factor is the person receiving the message lacks the background knowledge needed to understand the content of the message. Certain phrases or words require a certain degree of knowledge in order to understand it. Understanding the group who will be receiving the message can help the administrator with how the nature of the message should be written in order to help reduce the misunderstanding.

Social barriers
Social barriers the may deter from a message include factors such as age, sex and position in the hierarchy. Teachers who teach different subjects or grade levels may misinterpret the message. The same is true for men and women teachers as well as new and experienced teachers;

each one will develop their own interpretation of what the administrator was trying to say. Men and women each have their own way of communicating with others. Males can often be misinterpreted as arrogant or harsh whereas females can come across as weak and lack leadership. Different communication styles carry into the different cultures. Administrators should be aware of the different ways of communicating that may be inappropriate. Certain cultures may find it inappropriate to stand too close or to use a certain voice tone.

Interpersonal skills

Consensus building

After schools have determined what their educational needs are, then it is time to decide what the plans are to meet these needs and how they will be implemented. There will be many opinions and ideas from many people, and one way to decide what the best plan is, is through consensus building. Using this technique will allow everyone to have an opportunity to speak their opinion and have their voices heard. The goal is to persuade others to decide with a certain party. It is important that it is understood that everyone will get a chance to speak and their opinion will be respected even if others do not agree with it. Consensus is achieved when one party's viewpoint is preferred over the others. The one big disadvantage with this technique is that it can be extremely time consuming.

Using group consensus

Using groups to resolve conflict can be extremely resourceful to an administrator. Individuals in groups can provide a variety of opinions and offer creative ideas on how to resolve issues. It is important to first establish the rule that everyone's opinion will be valued and respected. If there are too many individuals involved, it could become a chaotic situation and nothing will be achieved, therefore, it is important for the administrator to keep order and structure. It may also be wise to keep the amount of people involved to a minimum. Once an idea has been agreed upon on how to solve an issue it is now time to decide on how to implement the plan. Everyone will have their own opinion but it is important for the group to come to an agreement on which plan best meets the needs of the school.

Conflict management technique

In most cases, when an administrator is deciding which technique is the most appropriate to resolve conflict, they would choose a contingency approach, which is choosing the technique based on the nature of the situation. However, an administrator should also consider the individual personal needs of the staff in selecting a conflict management technique. Other important factors to consider are the people involved in the conflict, how serious the situation is to them, the type and intensity of the conflict, and the authority that some individuals possess. An administrator is likely to encounter several different types of conflicts and therefore there will be a number of alternative techniques to choose from. One technique will not be suitable for all situations.

Leading the Schoolwide Educational Program

Student development and learning

Behaviorism

The theory of behaviorism states that if a new behavior pattern is repeated so many times it will become automatic. This theory is associated with the Russian physiologist, Pavlov. He performed an experiment on a dog. The dog would salivate when it saw food, so Pavlov would ring the bell seconds before he showed the dog his food; therefore, he trained the dog to salivate after hearing the ringing of the bell. Another famous psychologist associated with this theory is an American, John B. Watson. He performed an experiment on a young boy named Albert. Albert was initially not afraid of a white rat, but when the rat was shown to Albert along with a loud noise, he soon became afraid of the rat. Skinner is also associated with behaviorism except he studied operant behavior. According to his studies the learner behaves a certain way according to the environment.

Cognitivism

This theory states that learning involves using certain information that has been stored in the brain. One of the most famous psychologists associated with this theory is Jean Piaget. A key concept of the cognitive theory is schema; existing internal knowledge that has been stored in the brain and compared to new knowledge. There is also the three-stage information processing model, which means information is inputted through a sensory register, then is made into short-term memory and last is made into long-term memory and used for storage and retrieval. Other key concepts are a meaningful effect, which means information that has meaning is easier to remember and learn. Serial position effects mean that a person can remember items on a list if they start from the beginning or end. Some other effects that are associated with this theory are; practice, transfer, interference, organization, levels of processing, state dependent, mnemonic, schema, and advance organizers.

Constructivism

The theory of constructivism states that a person develops their own knowledge based on their past experiences. This theory states that each learner is unique because every learner comes from a different background and experiences. Social constructivism encourages the unique traits in each individual learner. The learner should become involved in the learning process; therefore, the responsibility of learning does not solely rest on the instructor. The learner will take and active role rather than be passive. This theory also states that the learning environment should be set up in order to challenge the learner to their full potential. The instructor's role is not to just give the information and answers according to a curriculum, but rather to encourage the learner the find conclusions and answers on their own. The goal for the instructor is to help the learners become effective thinkers and challenge themselves.

Principles of motivation

Administrators should have knowledge on individual behavior in order to understand why individuals are motivated to do the things they do. This includes individuals such as students, teachers and individuals in the community. Administrators should have knowledge on basic motivation because not everyone is motivated to do things in the same way. Different theorists have their theories on motivation. If an administrator wants something done, just telling that person to do something may not get the job done. Administrators need to have an understanding on how to reach out to people and motivate them to reach their full potential. It is important for an administrator to understand divergent behaviors as well, they need to know how to reach out and prevent certain activities without just telling individuals not to do something.

<u>Behavioral views of motivation</u>
There many behavioral learning theorists that have created techniques of behavior modification based on the idea that students arc motivated to complete an assignment because they have been promised a reward. This reward can be praise, a grade, a ticket that can be traded in for something else or it can be a privilege of selecting an activity of their choice. There are also operant conditioning interpretations that explain why some students like a certain subject while others have a strong dislike for it. For example, math, some students love it and others hate it. The students have love math, may have been brought up to love it. Their past experiences may have shaped them this way because they have all been positive. On the other hand, the students who hate math may have had negative experiences.

<u>Cognitive views of motivation</u>
Cognitive theorists believe people are motivated because their behavior is influenced by the way some think about themselves and the environment around them. This view of motivation is heavily influenced by Jean Piaget who developed the principles of equilibration, assimilation, accommodation and schema formation. He stated that children naturally want equilibration which means a sense of organization and balance in their world. The cognitive theorists also

believe that motivation comes from one's expectations for successfully completing a task. John Atkinson proposed motivation can also come from a person's desire for achievement. Some are high-need achievers and will seek out more challenging tasks, while others are low-need and will avoid challenging tasks. Those who avoid them do so because they have a fear of failure and that alone outweighs the expectation of success. William Glasser stated that for someone to be motivated to achieve success they must first experience success in some part of their lives.

<u>Humanistic view of motivation</u>
The humanistic view of motivation is heavily influenced by Abraham Maslow, most famous for Maslow's five-level hierarchy of needs. He proposed that everyone has five levels of needs and each level needs to be fulfilled first before moving on the next level. The bottom level is physiological needs, needs people need to survive, food, water, air and shelter. If this level is satisfied then people will be motivated to meet the needs of the next level, which is safety. After this level comes belongingness and love and after this level is esteem. These first four levels motivate people to act only when they are unmet to a certain point. The highest and last level is self-actualization, which is also called a growth need. Self-actualization is often referred to as a need for self-fulfillment. People come to this level because they have desire to fulfill their potential and capabilities.

Curriculum planning

<u>Curriculum objectives</u>
One of the most crucial steps an administrator needs to implement in order to have an effective school is to have clear goals and objectives for curriculum, instruction and learning outcomes. It is imperative to the school's

- 28 -

effectiveness that these goals are explained and well known to everyone that is involved with the student's learning. However, the goals can be well known but, how does an administrator know they are being achieved? One indicator of achievement is student assessment. Once the data has been collected on these an administrator can carefully examine the data and see if there are still weaknesses in the same areas or if there has been an improvement. Another indicator of achievement is the staff's opinions and attitudes. An open line of communication is crucial to any administrator wanting to achieve something more in their school. The staff can be able to tell if a curriculum is working or if there is still room for improvement.

Curriculum goals

Before an administrator can decide which curriculum to use or design it is important to first decide what the curriculum goals are going to be. These goals should not be determined by only the administrator but also the staff and parents. They should use data that has been collected through assessments and decide what the areas are that need improvement. It is crucial to ask teachers what they want out of a curriculum and in what direction do they want their students to go. Parents should also be asked what they expect their children to learn when they are at school. A curriculum should be based on a group effort. It should focus on what everyone wants the students to achieve and what is best for the school. Many times the district will already have goals and the school can just add to those.

Curriculum development

Functions of the state

The development of curriculum at the state level involves creating guidelines concerning the development and implementation of curricula and ways of assessing student achievement. The state also creates the tests and other performance measures that are required for each academic subject. They should take a limited approach and focus assessment on language arts, social studies, science and math. There has been a movement toward assessments to test the student's ability to complete projects and open-ended problem solving rather than the tradition pencil and paper methods. It is also the responsibility of the state to provide the needed material and resources to local school districts. Often times the most desired resources are monetary support and technical assistance. The state must also decide the graduation requirements in terms of credits and competencies. These functions are general and allow the district more ownership in deciding what their needs and strengths are.

Functions of the district

Each district can implement any program of study they feel is necessary for their schools, however, it would be to the district's advantage if the program is consistent for each grade level and uniform for each academic subject. If the district ensures a consistent and uniform program of study this would help guarantee equity that all students across the district are getting an equal education. Another advantage is it makes it easier for a student to transfer within the district. A parent will not have to worry that their child is not on the same level with other students simply because they changed schools. The school district should create a mastery core curriculum that will explain the subjects that all schools will offer. A mastery core will also explain the goals and objectives of each subject. However, there is still the freedom and flexibility for each school to development their curriculum using the mastery core for guidance.

Functions of the school

After the school has received the curriculum's goals and objectives from the state and district, it is time for the school to make choices. The school's decisions will be made under the leadership of the principal and teacher leaders. The school will also collect the appropriate input from parents and then build a curriculum that is guided by the mastery core. The school should identify their goals and needs and then supplement any classes they feel are necessary to add in order to meet the student's needs. As a team, there will be a decision about the schedule, curriculum integration, and how to align and implement the curriculum. If this process is to be successful, it is important that the principal has strong leadership skills and is well informed and active in the development process.

Curriculum options – Keep or renew. After there has been a decision on what the curriculum goals are it is time to make a decision on the curriculum. The administrator and staff basically have two choices to make; one is to keep the current curriculum and renew it or begin a new curriculum. It is best to renew a curriculum if there are minor adjustments that need to be made in order to improve student achievement. When choosing this option, the administrator and staff need to take a look at the curriculum and determine where improvements need to be made. The only improvements that may need to be made could be adding a new course or just implementing new activities. It is best to begin a new curriculum if the decision has been made to change of the focus of the learning experience and redesigning the school's educational goals.

Curriculum resources. Texts, software, and other media resources should be selected only after the mastery curriculum has been developed. Many times districts make the mistake of purchasing textbooks and then developing a curriculum based on the material that was purchased. Textbooks should only be used to enrich the curriculum not help to create it. Principals have a voice and influence in the district's selection process and should use their influence to ensure their school is getting the appropriate materials necessary to gain student achievement. One way of choosing appropriate texts is to read through the books and mark the page numbers that correspond to a certain objective. A principal can then choose the text that is the closest fit to the curriculum objectives and then discuss their findings with the selection committee.

After the curriculum guide has been created and all the necessary resource materials have been purchased, the district's testing office will develop a testing program. These tests will not duplicate or replace any of the state required tests; these will only be used as a supplement. A principal can use their leadership to ensure these tests do not take up too much time for administrators, teachers, and students. Many times districts will develop too many tests and it takes away time from the teacher to teach the students. Principals should also ensure that these tests do not require an excessive amount of monetary funds to develop, administer and score. The goal of these exams should be to provide educators and parents with information about student achievement and the results need to come in a form that everyone can understand. Principals who want to have an influence on the district testing program should focus on these concerns.

The state has a crucial and legitimate role in the development of the curriculum frameworks and a principal can be proactive and get involved with the foundation documents while they are being developed. An effective principal should use their influence at the state level in order to achieve what they think is best for their school. In order to achieve this, principals need to stay informed about new ideas that the state may be developing. Knowing in advance what the situation is, is better than trying to react to what is already happening. The state professional association is a great source of information. It is also important the principal knows how the legislative process operates formally and informally. Also, if a principal wants to have a voice in what they believe in, then they need to be knowledgeable of the latest facts and research information. The best source is going to be professional journals.

Instructional resources. When an administrator is deciding what the curriculum needs are, he or she has several resources they can turn to. One of the best resources is the personnel. The teachers and teacher aides are vital to this decision. They are the ones teaching the curriculum and they are experts at knowing what additional needs there are. They will know if there needs to be more activities or if there should be an integration of another curriculum. There could also be a need of more materials. Many times there is a material shortage and not enough for each teacher to give to the students. The finances are another useful resource to use. Administrators need to be extremely careful and use the finances wisely when it comes to curriculum. Advisory groups, community agencies, and institutions can also be extremely resourceful when deciding the needs. These can give their opinion on what they think will best for the students.

Functions of the classroom
After the state, district and school have performed their functions concerning curriculum, now it is time for the classroom teachers to enhance the curriculum using their personal style. The

teachers can carry out the curriculum either as an individual or as a member of team or department. This is an opportunity for the teachers to develop yearly calendars and from there develop specific units of study based on the calendar. When making a yearly calendar this allows for the teachers to plan activities ahead of time, for example field trips or guest speakers. This is a time when a teacher can enrich the curriculum by using their own unique style of teaching that meets the needs of the students. Teachers know the students best and know when there is an area that needs to be taught in a certain way in order to gain student achievement.

Integrating curriculum. There are ways to integrate curriculum and still maintain separate subjects. One way is correlation, which means the school can have two subjects that use a curriculum in a way that they support each one of the two subjects. For example, if students are reading literature from a certain era, then in social studies students are studying events that occurred in that same era. Another way to integrate is using skills across the curriculum. All the skills involving reading, writing, social studies, science and math are reinforced throughout the curriculum. There is also the unified curriculum, which means the curriculum of a particular subject and its divisions are focused more on the overall objectives and not divided. The last way is informal integration, which means the teacher can simultaneously bring in content from one curriculum while emphasizing another.

Holistic approach. The holistic approach to curriculum development focuses on the student's way of thinking that is affected by each student's surrounding environment. Students use their culture and environment to help create knowledge. When using this approach, the curriculum planning is based on the developmental needs and interests of the children. Teachers do not follow a certain program, but rather they observe and take notes about what the students are conversing about. They pay attention to what the interests are of the students and share this information with other team members in order to develop appropriate learning activities. If the students share a common interest then this may be built into a thematic lesson that helps the students explore and investigate this interest. The project can include many skills such as writing, reading, singing, painting and mathematics and involve using small groups.

Effective instruction

Principles of instruction
There have been times when the principles of effective instruction have been described as art and not something taught to teachers in college. A teacher must possess certain qualities about themselves in order for their instruction to be effective. One quality is the teacher must show an honest interest and enthusiasm for the subject they are teaching. If the teacher is not interested the students won't be either. In the classroom they must also show respect and interest in each student. The students should be allowed time to ask questions and discuss with others about the subject matter. The objectives should be clear and the students should know what is expected of them. Any class activities, homework or projects should reflect what has been discussed in class and graded appropriately and fairly. The tests and papers should accurately measure what has been accomplished through the course objectives.

Instructional objectives
Instructional objectives are very specific and describe what the student is expected to do. Therefore, it is important that when deciding what the objectives are going to

be, teachers and administrators know exactly what they expect from their students. Instructional objectives are also determined by what the outcome will be. They will state what the student should be able to accomplish after the teacher has finished his or her instruction. It is important to make sure the objectives are used to ensure that learning is clearly focused on a goal and that both students and teacher are on the same track. When determining instructional objectives, it is also important to ensure they line up with the lesson plan. It does not make sense for a teacher to teach a lesson on a certain topic, but the objectives do not follow the same topic.

Instructional methods

Many factors need to be considered before a teacher chooses a particular instructional method. Many excellent teachers have acquired the ability to use and transition from one method to the other. One factor to consider is the age of the students. Some methods may work better with younger children than with older and vice versa. Teachers should also consider the developmental level of their students. Another factor to consider is the number of students and the space available. Certain methods just work better with a smaller group while others work best with larger groups. There can be times when the number of students is appropriate; however, the space may not be available. One of the most important considerations is to pick a method that will best reflect the instructional objectives. There is not a "best" method for teaching, it is just important to consider all factors and pick the one that fits best at that time.

Contract method
The contract method involves writing a contract between the student and teacher that outlines what the student is to learn, what the grade will be and how it will be

learned. The teacher and student sign it and it is agreed that the student is responsible for achieving the goals that were stated in the contract. This method allows for the student for self directing. The student feels more empowered and takes ownership in their learning. They feel like they have the ability to teach themselves and still depend on the teacher for a backup. The contract method can also be used for behavioral changes as well. This method is not used in many schools. It should also only be used with students who are of the appropriate age and who are going to take it seriously. This is a big responsibility to put on a student it and the students chosen should be chosen wisely.

Cooperative learning method

Cooperative learning models are becoming more popular in the school systems. This type of learning model states that students are more likely to gain achievement if they are working as a member in a small group. Many schools are accepting this learning style because it is also the same model that many corporations use. Groups are formed and each group is responsible for a certain goal. However, each student in a group is also responsible for some part. Everyone must prove they have participated and learned something. Therefore, it is extremely important that the teacher is certain that every student knows what the concepts and goals are. After the teacher has given each task, then they come together to work on solving that task together.

Direct teaching

When a teacher chooses the direct teaching method he or she must have complete knowledge of the subject and content taught. He or she should have good oral communication skills. All the content used for teaching needs to be organized in advance. The learning objectives and goals are very specific and the students are told exactly why the learning material is important. Using this method makes it easier for the teacher to measure student achievement. The direct teaching method is also widely accepted and it is good for teaching specific facts and basic skills. However, there are some disadvantages. This method does not allow for the teacher to express his or her creativity. Material needs to be followed in a precise order. This method is not particularly helpful with higher-order thinking skills.

Group instruction

Group instruction involves all the students hearing the learning material at the same time. The teacher gives instruction, directions and explanations to everyone at once. This method is useful if it used at small increments during the day. The disadvantage to this method is there are students who benefit better with more individualized attention. They could get lost in the instruction. Group instruction can also be given in small groups, called small group instruction. This method allows the students to get more individualized attention from the teacher. It is also an opportunity for the teacher is examine how well each student is learning the material. It is important that while the teacher is involved with small groups the other students are actively engaging in other activities. If they are not they could cause a distraction to other students who are receiving small group instruction.

Individualized instruction

Individualized instruction involves the teacher carefully examining a student and deciding which instructional method is best to use with that student. Every student is different and their learning style is different. If a student is struggling and needs more one on one attention, then it is the responsibility of the teacher to make sure that student gets what they need. Finding the right instructional method may take a few times to get it right, it may be helpful to get the parents involved and ask them which way they think the student will learn best. Individualized instruction caters to that particular student and it is needed for student achievement. This method makes sure that student is getting their educational needs met in order for that student to achieve success.

Interdisciplinary approach

The interdisciplinary approach is used to encourage learning across the curriculum. Lessons are set up to make thematic units in all learning subjects. Each subject will be connected to this thematic unit. The teacher is making links between each subject. When this method is used the student is able to learn without fragments during day and at the same time have a stimulating learning experience. The teacher chooses a topic or theme and then brainstorms activities to do in each subject area that revolve around this topic. Questions are then thought of in order to serve as the scope and sequence. The teacher can determine a grade by evaluating standards of performance levels or by using rubrics that evaluate the students completed work assignments.

Team teaching

The team teaching method has been used at many grade levels in many different schools. Different schools may use this method in different ways; there is no correct way to use team teaching. This method involves the students switching classes and having different teachers throughout the day. Team teaching can be divided by subjects, where the student has a different teacher for each subject. It can also be divided by just two teachers, in this situation one teacher may take math and science and the other will take language arts and social studies. If this method is chosen it is important that the

teachers have good communication between each other. The teachers should make sure the goals are the same. Team teaching fails when there is no communication and a lack of respect and honesty exists.

Instructional strategies

Author's Chair

The Author's Chair is a strategy that allows students to share with other students the writing work they have created on their own. This is the final step in the writing process. A special time is created for the student to read aloud their final product with the audience and then receive feedback from their classmates. The feedback is beneficial for the writer and audience because both of these parties can improve their writing. It is important that the teacher stresses that comments from both the author and audience are respectful and accepting. This process is used to help students realize their ideas are worthy of sharing and to develop their sense of authorship. It also enhances the student's listening and attention span skill, for the ones who are apart of the listening audience.

Drill and practice

Drill and practice is a very familiar instructional strategy to many teachers. This method uses repetitive practices of specific skills in order for students to retain the information. It is often used for the memorization of spelling words and math problems. In order for drill and practice to be effective, it must be used with appropriate strategies to develop certain competencies. Many times teachers use this method for beginning learners or for certain students who may be experiencing learning problems. This method should be used only if the teacher is absolutely certain that it is the most appropriate form of instruction to use. There are software packages that can be purchased for the use of drill and practice.

It is important to use the ones that provide feedback to students as to why they got an answer correct or incorrect.

Guided reading and thinking

The guided reading and thinking strategy is a way for the teacher to guide a student's comprehension of a reading selection by asking the students questions. The focus of this instructional form is to use context to predict meaning. The purpose is to help students develop story sense and to help students learn the purposes for reading. Comprehension is acquired by helping students use their past experiences and knowledge of language. One way teachers can use this method is by having the students predict what the story is going to be about by just looking at the cover and reading the title. Then, their guesses can be listed in a story grid or outline. While reading, teachers should stop and ask the students questions about the story and compare what is happening compared to their predictions. Assessments and evaluations can be made by assessing the student's abilities to comprehend certain types of texts.

Learning activities

When choosing learning activities that reflect the instructional objectives, it is important to remember that these activities should encourage students to have meaningful interaction between other students and the instructor. Activities can include anything from writing papers, doing projects, group discussion and hands on activities. It may be difficult for the teacher to decide which activity is best; therefore after deciding the instructional objectives, a teacher should keep them near by and use them as a source for deciding which activity to use. There are different levels of objectives and the instructor will want to choose the activity or activities based on that particular level. It is important to remember that what ever activity is

chosen, it must support the student in learning the instructional objectives. It must also align with what the lesson is about.

Scaffolding

The instructional technique, scaffolding, is a process where the teacher models how to perform a certain learning strategy and then the responsibility gradually shifts to the students. Scaffolding is intended to be temporary because some of the work is being done for the students who are not ready to complete the task by themselves. Teachers can perform this strategy by modeling the task and thinking out loud in either direct of indirect instruction. A teacher can adapt this instructional technique by pairing students up according to development level or by engaging students with cooperative learning. Students can help other students in the cooperative learning style; however, teacher assistance is still needed. A teacher can assess the students by using anecdotal notes, student self assessment or by using graphic organizers. These types of organizers are a scaffolding tool that visually represents an idea.

Development and evaluation of classroom tests

When an administrator helps a teacher develop and evaluate more valid tests it will give both them more confidence that the data gathered from these are accurate and reliable. The teacher will then want to analyze what information was taught to the students and then decide what objectives will be tested. Obviously, not every objective can be tested so it is important to pick the objectives that have the most significance. The teacher will need to decide what the weight will be for each objective; this is a way for the teacher to score the test. Once those decisions are made then it is time for the teacher to decide how each question will be asked. There a variety of ways to ask a question; multiple choice, essay form, true/false or fill in the blank. The next step is to organize how the questions will be listed and then write the directions. Teachers should ensure the directions are written clearly so that the students have a clear understanding of what is expected.

Assessments for strategizing

One way to determine instructional strategies and priorities is to examine the assessments of student achievement. Student assessments give administrators and instructors a chance to see on what level the students are achieving or struggling. If students are struggling in a certain area then it is time to decide if a certain teaching method needs to be changed or adjusted in some way. Priorities also need to be set in regards to deciding what teaching methods need to be changed and which ones work best with what student. If the assessments show students are achieving in certain areas, then administrators will know certain methods are successful. Priorities should be set on how to decide continuing with this achievement. The instructors should be asked if they need any additional materials to continue on this road to success.

Level of achievement assessments
Assessing students allows administrators and teachers to understand at what level their students are on, whether it is reading, math, science or social studies. Assessments can give an indication of what area students are achieving and in what areas they are struggling. If there is an area of great achievement then administrators can take that information and decide what exactly it is that this school is doing right in order to get these results. They can also ask themselves if there is anything else this school needs in order to help students keep achieving in a particular area. The same is true if after

an assessment there is an area where students are struggling. Administrators can look at this data and ask why are students struggling and what are the needs that need to be met in order to achieve improvement. After all this data has been collected and needs have been identified then administrators can start setting priorities to ensure improvement will be made.

Performance assessment method
There has been a growing trend of teachers complaining about assessing students through the traditional pencil and paper method. Many teachers have been trying to encourage a new trend of assessing through student performance. A student would be asked to perform a task in order to demonstrate their competence of a certain objective. Administrators can help teachers with this type of assessment by providing encouragement and supporting new ideas of assessment activities. Administrators must first help teachers decide the major educational goal they want students to be able achieve at the end of a marked time of the school year. Next, the administrator and teacher should decide what behaviors the students should be able to demonstrate regarding this goal. Then, a decision should be made about which academic activities best will represent what the students have learned regarding this objective.

Accountability

Effective administrators know the importance of building a school community including, teachers, parents and students. When all of these groups are actively involved it will increase student achievement. However, it is vital to hold teachers accountable for their teaching. They can be held accountable by having to show their lesson plans, exhibit examples of student work and they can clearly define the goals of the school and in their classroom. Administrators should express to them clearly that this is what is expected of them. Without effective teaching learning will be diminished and possibly disappear. Administrators can help teachers be accountable by providing them with necessary materials and always be willing to provide them support and encouragement. Teachers need to feel they are important and their voices and concerns are heard.

Role of technology

Today's classrooms still consistent of the constructivist way of teaching, which is the teacher sharing their knowledge of a subject and the students are expected to remember everything and then be able to demonstrate what they know on a standardized test. An effective administrator should be trying to find ways to use technology as a tool to enhance the constructivist way of teaching. Technology should not be used as a substitute for teaching, but as a way to enhance today's learning. Technology can also provide professional growth by enhancing a teacher's way of teaching. This could be a difficult change for many teachers, especially the ones who are accustomed to the constructivist ways of teaching. However, a teacher will want to avoid an excessive use of technology because the students may loose that personal relationship with the teacher.

Technology implementation
When deciding which technological equipment to use in a school, the principal serves as the major decision maker. It is their responsibility to ensure the staff receives adequate training regarding all new equipment and they must arrange usage agreements with businesses and other educational institutions. A teacher cannot be expected to implement technology in the classroom if they do not know how to use it. It is also the responsibility of the principal to show full support of newly implemented technology. Many times they may have to market the program to the staff in order for the staff to be supportive of it. If a principal can clearly state how new technology can benefit not only the students but the staff as well, it will increase the likely hood of the staff accepting it.

Teacher's role
In order for a student to be successful the teacher needs to create an environment that creates engaged learning. One role is a facilitator. When an administrator is observing a teacher who is effectively being an administrator he or she will observe the teacher being interactive with students using computers or other technology in the classroom. The teacher will also provide and opportunity for the students to collaborate with each other and to share their knowledge. When a teacher is acting as the role of guide, he or she is modeling and coaching a certain task. This teacher will know how to adjust the level of information based on the needs of the students. They are able to help the students learn by connecting their prior knowledge with new knowledge. There is also the role of co-learner and co-investigator. In this situation the teacher creates learning situations involving professionals.

Gender and technology
There has been a common trend in the educational system that boys are favored over girls in the area of technology. It is the responsibility of the administrator to ensure girls get the same opportunities as boys when it comes to technology. It is important that girls feel that the same opportunities are available to them as the boys and are given a chance to pursue interests in computers and engineering. The goal is to have an equal-opportunity environment for both genders and others with special needs. There could be many situations where girls in a particular

school truly do not have an interest in technology; however they should be given a chance to use technology in subjects they are interested in. Technology can be integrated in history, language arts, music and many other subjects.

Positive school culture

Supportive environment
In order for a school to be a productive learning environment, the principal must create and maintain a positive environment. One way this can be achieved is by building a school culture. Building a school culture means building a team of parents, teachers and students. This culture knows what the core values of the school are and are motivated to fulfill these values. These values are things such as clear expectations of the students, holding students accountable for following school rules and turning in assignments. Everyone knows these values because the principal knows how to communicate them effectively. An effective principal who wants to build a culture knows the importance of repeating, explaining and discussing these values to everyone. They also know that once these values have been communicated to the team members, they keep building this culture based on the strengths and values of every member.

Symbolism
It is important that the entire school community understand the expectations and sanctions of the school. These can be communicated through symbolism and can be done in the form of a slogan, group rituals or awards banquet. Values and expectations can also be communicated by symbolic activity through behavioral change. If students are expected to act in a certain way then staff members and the administrator should be expected to perform that same behavior. The goal of symbolic activity is not what is said but rather what actions are taken to reflect the desired behavior. If students are expected to read then they should see teachers reading. Administrators should also apply this strategy for staff members. If something is expected of them then as the leader, the administrator should demonstrate the behavior as well.

High standards and expectations
When a school focuses on school culture it helps to improve the child's total development. This involves the development of social, moral, physical and psychological skills. When a culture is brought together everyone is working together as a team to make sure every child is getting a quality education. The same values are shared and are communicated to everyone, especially the students. Therefore, the students know what is expected of them. These values can be communicated through symbolic actions, such as a sign or slogan. They can also be communicated through positive and negative sanctions. The goal is to have more positive sanctions, for example recognizing student achievement. Research has shown that more positive reinforcement can overcome the negative. However, if a student is not meeting the expectations and causing trouble, then negative sanction will be necessary.

When an administrator is striving to build a school culture it is important to have certain characteristics. School culture consists of everyone; teachers, students, parents and other staff members. One of these important traits is paying attention to the values of its members. These are the ideas and opinions of the member and what they feel is needed for the improvement of the school. One sign of an effective culture is the behavior of the members, whether or not they are positive and upbeat. Another sign is whether or not teachers are interacting with students and parents in a positive and effective way and vice versa. A strong culture also respects the written and

- 38 -

unwritten policies and procedures. In order for the administrator to truly understand the school's culture they should take the time and perform group interviews, this way they can accurately understand the issues of the school.

Building character. One of the many responsibilities of an administrator is building the character of the students. They should always set high expectations for good behavior in the lives of the students. However, if students are expected to behave and act in a certain way then they must see examples of good behavior happening in the environment around them. What happens at home cannot be controlled but what happens at school can. Students should be able to see staff members using caring words and having a positive attitude. Changing student's attitudes can have a major impact on their work habits and achievement. Character building is something that can be carried with a student for the rest of their life. Responsibility, kindness, caring, trustworthiness, and integrity are character traits students will need as they continue on through school and adulthood it does not stop in elementary school.

Emphasizing academic achievement. If administrators want an effective school then there must be an emphasis on academic effort and achievement. There should still be an emphasis on student behavior and character building; however, effective schools stress effort and achievement with the highest priority. Ways of communicating these to the community is through a mission statement, educational goals or printing them on documents. Another effective way of communicating that effort and achievement as top priority is through the staff member's attitudes. Effective schools have everyone adopting the attitudes that the students are capable of high

achievement. If students have someone that truly believes in them, then they will start to believe in themselves. Teachers should also adopt the attitude for themselves; that they can help each student in their class reach their full potential.

Appropriate levels. An administrator should set high expectations regarding students. However, it is important for the administrator to remember every student is different and the expectations should be set accordingly. One of the first considerations to take is the student's developmental level. An administrator needs to be aware if the student has any learning disabilities or is developmentally slow. Expectations should not be set too high especially if the expectations are not developmentally appropriate for the students. Another factor to consider is the instructional level for the students. Expectations should not be set so high that they go beyond the instructional level. A kindergartener can not be expected to perform on the same level as a sixth grader. The opposite is also true; expectations should not be set too low that the students will be performing below grade level and not want to achieve anything higher than that.

Building school culture

Before an administrator can enhance a school culture, he or she must first achieve a good understanding and full knowledge of what the organizational culture is. After this has been achieved then the administrator can move on to the next step of enhancing it. If the school culture is not an effective one, it will be a challenge for the administrator to change it. The administrator must envision the future of the school, what is the goal that will make the school improve. An administrator must also make it a priority to meet the needs of the teachers and students. Enhancing the school culture will more likely be achieved if the administrator views a problem as an opportunity to find solutions not another burden. It will also be enhanced if teachers are encouraged to use creative practices and they are given opportunities to share their ideas and made to fill they are a vital part of the improvement of the school. The most important factor that will enhance school culture is staying focused on student achievement.

Subcultures and countercultures
It is well known that effective administrators know how to shape and lead an effective school culture. Administrators can easily get the impression that the school is under one culture. This is highly unlikely because of each school will contain a wide variety of personalities and opinions. A school can have multiple organizations that make up a culture, subculture and even countercultures and each one is the one who wants to define who the school is. The most common example of this is in secondary schools where there are several departments and subjects. Many of the departments make up a culture and possibly within the department are subcultures. This can be an extremely difficult challenge for an administrator trying to understand and gather information about the school's culture and trying to set goals and expectations.

Leadership conflicts
Any time when leaders of the school are different people, there is a strong potential for conflict. There could be a disagreement on a wide variety of topics, and any type of conflict could make it harder on the administrator to build a unified organizational culture. The important issue an administrator needs to remember is to listen effectively to both sides in order to understand the main issue of the conflict. There should be an opportunity for both the formal and

informal leader to be able to voice their opinion and ensure they feel they are important. An administrator can use their influence to persuade one party into the direction that is more suitable to the overall school organizational culture, however this may not work every time. There is not a correct way of handling a situation like this; however, an administrator with strong conflict resolution skills can change a difficult situation.

Faculty

Creating learning communities
One important role an administrator must fulfill is bringing the staff together as a team and help create a learning community. A learning community is created when the team shares the same mission, vision and values. It should be clearly known that the goal is about helping students reach their full potential. When everyone knows what the goals are then the whole team is striving for the same thing. It is also important that different grade levels work collaboratively in reaching their goals. Each staff member should strive toward continuous improvement. Goals may be accomplished in small increments but it is important to keep focused and never lose sight of what the mission is. If a problem arises then everyone comes together and develops an action plan to solve the issue.

Encouraging communication
An effective administrator knows the importance of encouraging communication at every level throughout the school organization. In most cases there is communication from principal to staff but not from staff to principal. It is important that an administrator encourages staff members to communicate with them and convey the importance of their opinions. In order for a staff member to communicate effectively with the principal they must

feel they are important and their ideas, opinions and feelings are valuable to the school. There will be a decrease of communication if staff members feel what they are saying is not important and there is no sense of trust and respect. In order to gain this trust, a principal may realize there is a need to develop strategies to build organizational and personal trust.

Staff relationships

The entire school community must work together as a team, under the leadership of the administrator, in order to have student achievement. The administrator must remember their role as a leader. An effective administrator knows the importance of treating the staff with respect and dignity. All staff should feel they play an important role in the school and their opinions and values matter. An administrator must also treat the staff equitably and fairly. When a staff is treated with fairness, respect and dignity there is a stronger desire to perform at a higher level. Any situation where there is conflict should be dealt with professionally and with fairness. It is also important that administrators know the importance of interacting with their staff not only professionally but personally as well as long as it does not cause to treats others more favorably.

Referent influence

If an administrator possesses a referent influence, this means others are able to identify with the administrator as a person. Certain characteristics that others can identify with are a strong character, outspoken personality and compelling leadership style. Characteristics like these may enable an administrator to gain cooperation from others even if teachers, parents and students may question the decisions made by the administrator. The qualities are positive and tend to make people want to react positively to another. However, there are no certain types of character traits that have a

positive impact on everyone. While some groups respond positively to certain traits others may view them as a sign of weak leadership. Another issue with referent influence is that if an administrator is in a position of leadership, their authenticity has already been established, and if certain traits are not there, then the probability of them developing is unlikely.

Reward influence

This type of influence means an administrator has certain rewards that can be given out to certain individuals who act and obey certain decisions an administrator makes. One issue with this type of influence it that an administrator may not have enough rewards to be able to distribute equally. There may occasionally be a time when rewards may be offered to an individual or group without having to distribute the same reward to others. However, this may seem like preferential treatment and in the education field this is not viewed favorably. Another problem that may arouse is the administrator may receive very little rewards to give from the school board and other bureaucratic agencies. Although these problems may occur, an administrator can develop their own variety of awards. These rewards can include a free period, an additional lunch break or support a new activity a teacher wants to implement.

Positive reinforcement

One reward that an administrator has an abundant amount of and is often overlooked is positive reinforcement. This reward can be given out in the form of written or verbal communication. Taking the time out of the day to go to a teacher or other staff member and tell them they are doing a great job can have a major impact. Many times an administrator may think they are already giving out plenty of positive reinforcement, but in fact they are not. Any administrator can give positive reinforcement, but an effective one knows that reinforcement must be clearly related to a certain task the staff member is doing. If compliments are given out randomly, then they seem meaningless and not valued as much and in return the behavior that is desired may not occur.

Empowerment

Leadership does not just involve one person; it involves empowering others to contribute to making decisions and working together to achieve the school's goals. Administrators can empower the staff by allowing them to make decisions and express their opinions. When others feel as though they have voice and they matter, there will be an increase in their desire to achieve the school's goals. One way an administrator can empower the staff is by rewarding them for their success. An administrator can also empower the staff by using words of encouragement and letting them know how much they are appreciated. It is also important that administrators build excitement in teaching and express their pride in the teachers. Empowerment can also come in the form of the administrator's own behavior and how they interact with their superiors.

Empowering teachers
When administrators empower teachers they allow them to have a voice in the decision making process. This makes them feel valued and in return will improve their performance. Administrators are still the leaders and facilitate the school goals and encourage teachers to create their own ideas. However, the more power teachers have the more responsibility they will have to take the burden for. Administrators should make it be clearly known that each teacher is solely responsible for carrying out their duties and performing them to the best of their ability. However, administrators should be responsible for

providing the necessary training and education for each teacher that informs them of the appropriate decision making skills. In order to make this empowerment successful the school board members have to be in support of it as well.

Supervising staff development

An effective administrator realizes that teachers do not know how to do everything on their own. There needs to be critical training for each teacher however, not every teacher needs help in every area. Setting staff development priorities should be based on the staff's needs. These staff developments need to be arranged to improve the teacher's skills in a particular area. This is extremely important, especially if the school is implementing a new program. The teachers should not be expected to know how to teach it without the proper training. Many times teachers feel as though staff development is something they have to go to in order to fulfill their staff development requirements. These training times should not be something they have to go to, these should be times when teachers actually find ways to improve their teaching skills. Priorities should be set according to what is important for the school.

Assessing staff abilities
Administrators should assess staff abilities to find their strengths and to find ways to keep encouraging those strengths. An effective administrator is a mentor and has the ability to encourage their staff and make them believe in themselves. An assessment can also give an administrator an opportunity to determine what the staff's needs are. Some teachers may need more material because there is a shortage. Others may need more support and encouragement. After assessment is not a time to pick on the weak, it is a time to bring up the ones

- 42 -

who need help by offering guidance. In order to have an effective school year, the entire school needs to come together and work as a team. Making sure the staff's needs are met will help ensure that the student's needs are met and in return there will be student achievement.

Teacher training

In a school based management, the training teachers receive can be delivered in a variety of ways. The funding for these training sessions is also varied; the funding can come from statewide professional organizations, sometimes grants or diverting funds from other areas. Many times schools will use their surplus of funds to send teachers to training or make cut backs in other areas and then use that money for training. Many statewide professional organizations or foundations will help sponsor teacher training or provide support. In most cases the district will hold district wide workshops for teachers and other staff members. The instructors for these workshops can be hired consultants or a fellow staff member trained to lead a workshop. There can be times when the school districts will vary on how much discretion they have in selecting a type of training program.

In almost all school districts staff development is a requirement for teachers and other staff members. These training sessions are usually decided by central-office staff and they decide which sessions will best fit the needs of the school. These members may or may not have even visited any of the schools and therefore do not know the needs of the school or its teachers. Schools that encourage teachers and administrators to work together to develop staff development training sessions can decide which ones best meet the needs of the school and the goals. If teachers and other staff members feel they have an opinion

in deciding the training sessions, they will have a greater sense of responsibility and feel they are contributing to the improvement of the school. Teachers may also take a greater interest in the sessions and not feel they are made to go in order to fulfill a requirement.

Development activities
In order for a school to achieve success, an administrator should involve each teacher in the planning and implementation of staff development activities. Staff development activities not only enhance a teacher's skills but it is also a tool to get other teachers to help each other. An administrator's responsibility is to help teachers assess their needs and ensure they have the necessary tools and support to carry out their duties. Staff development activities can provide wonderful ideas to enhance student achievement, however, if a teacher does not have the necessary material to perform these lessons, then goal will be harder to achieve. Administrators should also provide each teacher with classroom management and teaching models of these activities. This may make it easier for the teacher to perform them instead of just hearing about them during one staff development session.

Effective content. Effective staff development programs focus on school improvement and not how to improve the teachers. If staff development programs are to be effective, they need to focus on what the assessed needs are of the ones who are participating. The content of the programs should be focused on improving specific skills and not developing new concepts. Teachers can often feel overwhelmed with the introduction of new concepts every time they attend a staff development workshop. It is best if the teachers can relate to the content because of their prior experiences. Teachers should also be able to see a demonstration of the strategic model that is to be implemented. Many times teachers are told how to perform a technique but never shown and in return it fails. Modeling it may not be satisfactory enough for all teachers, there should be a follow up to help with the implementation of a new skill.

Technology training

The principal's role as technology leader is to provide the staff with the appropriate training in technology in order to enhance their teaching skills. Many times teachers are required to attend a two hour workshop and are not given enough opportunities to practice or get feedback. It is important to remember that if a new technology is to be implemented, teachers need to be given the appropriate support and supervision during the time of implementation. One of the main reasons programs fail is because the teachers are given the information in handouts about a program but are given no help on how to do it, therefore, they return to the old practices. An effective administrator provides the necessary resources to the teachers in order for them to be successful and in return help the students become successful.

Evaluating teacher workshops

Workshops are used to improve the skills of teachers. However, these workshops and other programs should be evaluated in order to ensure their effectiveness. Evaluating a workshop can provide useful information to the agencies that fund these workshops, the institutions that sponsor them, the instructors and the participants. Evaluations can show if the participants found it was a worthy program and where improvements need to be made. The instructor of the workshop can gather a variety of information such as how to plan the class, decide the procedures for running the workshop, deciding on the most effective activities and making changes if there

needs to be any. An effective evaluation should be done during the program, at the end of certain parts of the program and at the end of the program. A formative evaluation can be used to make changes during the program while a summative evaluation can be used to assess how well participants have met the goals.

Teacher evaluation

The purpose of teacher evaluations is to measure teacher competence and help the teacher in their professional development. The evaluation system should also serve as means of receiving feedback on their classroom needs and to learn other teaching methods. Certain standards should be set in order to achieve these goals, such as standards that relate to the teaching skills that are important. Each teacher should have these standards clearly expressed to them before and after an evaluation and they should be linked to the professional development of the teacher. When an administrator is evaluating they should consider a variety of teaching skills and not just one. A more accurate evaluation includes other sources of information about the teacher's performance other than a time 45 minute stay in the classroom.

Formal/Informal evaluations

Evaluations are set up to determine teacher competence and to foster professional growth and development. Evaluations is a time for a teacher to receive useful feedback about classroom needs, ideas on new teaching techniques, and advice on how to make useful changes in the classroom. Administrators can perform informal evaluations by having a "walk through," which the administrator may only observe a teacher for a few minutes and may or may not take notes. Formal evaluations are a time when the administrator will observe the teacher for a longer period of time and make assessments. The administrator will be observing classroom activities, review lesson plans and classroom records and observe how the students are reacting to the lesson. This information is recorded and is compared to certain domain requirements the teacher should fulfill. A post-observation will follow and the administrator will deliver the feedback about their strengths and weaknesses.

Using a teacher portfolio

A teacher portfolio is a tool that can be used to collect work produced by a teacher that expresses their talents, knowledge and skills in teaching. Some items that can be included in the portfolio are the teacher's background, what subjects they teach, any state exams that have been taken, and the teacher's personal statement about what it means to teach. These portfolios can be used as a mean of assessment or to provide feedback to teachers on ways they can improve their teaching. If an administrator wants teachers to implement a portfolio program, it is important for him or her to remember these take time and a teacher needs to start slowly. It is important that both teachers and administrators support the use of portfolios because either the program will fail or no one will put forth the effort to make it work.

Post-evaluation meeting

After a teacher evaluation, it is necessary for the administrator and teacher to have post evaluation meeting. This is a time when the positive and negative evaluation findings will be discussed. It is important that the administrator remember they are a leader and leaders build up members of their team and not bring them down. The positive findings should be highlighted first and then the negative. This is a time to set goals for any improvements that may need to be made. If there are any changes that need to be made, then resources need to be offered that can help with the improvement. Resources can be books, research findings or assigning a mentor teacher to someone who needs one. Evaluations should be used as a tool to find any changes that need to be made in order to gain student achievement.

Evaluation concerns

Even the most experienced teachers may have concerns that evaluations are not productive and do not show the teacher's full capabilities. One concern is that the evaluation criterion is decided by others, such as state laws and school boards, and teachers do not have enough input. Another concern is the length of time an evaluator will spend in the classroom Many times an evaluator will come in for about 45 minutes and that is the only time that evaluator will spend in that classroom the whole school year. In that short period of time, a teacher may feel not enough quality information has been gathered. Teachers are also concerned that the evaluator is not properly trained and may have little experience teaching in a classroom. They also feel the results of the evaluations do not help to further teacher development or any program for professional development.

Program evaluation

An administrator needs to be aware of problems associated with the implementation of a new program before these problems become a major crisis. A formative evaluation can represent assessments of the programs strengths and areas that need improvement before a decision is made whether or not the program is successful. In the early stages of a new program this type of evaluation can be resourceful because this is the time when unanticipated problems are more likely to occur. In order to prevent the problems from becoming a crisis, immediate action may be needed. The most important goal of a formative evaluation is that it provides the administrator with enough information on the progress of the implementation of a program. After the information has been gathered, there should not be a decision to discontinue the program at that time. The implementation process should be given enough time to improve itself before that decision is made.

Summative evaluations

A summative evaluation provides valuable information concerning whether or not a new program is meeting the school or school district objectives. This type of evaluation requires the collection of data and subjective judgments on what the data means. The kinds of summative evaluations that may be required are comparisons of student behavior, achievement, and attitudes before and after the implementation of the new program. It would also be resourceful to collect data on the teacher and parent attitudes before and after the implementation process. In order to collect this data, it is important to consider what is to be evaluated, what information is needed and what method is most appropriate. There is no method that is the correct one; there is a variety to choose from, questionnaires, interviews or content analysis. If administrators choose not to assess a new program then other stakeholders may make their own assessments using their own methods and opinions.

Managing School Resources, Finances, and Compliance

Theories, principles and practices

Organization defined

An organization is a group that sets their own goals, develops ways of pursuing those goals and controls their own performance. According to a sociology perspective an organization is planned and coordinated by human beings in order to produce a certain product. The organization is an arrangement of certain elements and these elements are determined by rules in order to complete a task. This task is completed by individuals through division of labor. The elements are considered to be the individuals in the organization and how each one communicates with the other. If the elements are coordinated and planned appropriately with everyone's cooperation the organization is given the abilities to solve tasks that will be given to them. The benefit of organizations is there are more enhancements because of the different features of each element.

Complexity theory

The complexity theory is used in the domain of strategic management and organizational studies in order to understand how organizations can adapt to their environments. When the organization is able to share similar properties of their environment, then they are more likely to survive. This type of complexity theoretic thinking has also been used in strategy and organizational studies. There has been recent work done on this theory that has added to the understanding of how concepts from the complexity sciences can be used to understand organizational studies and strategic management. Other theorists such as Karl Weick have used this theory for his loose coupling theory and interest in causal dependencies.

Marxist theory

The Marxist theorists believe that organizations are created to benefit managerial control rather than achieve efficiency. They also believe workers are stripped of their skills in order to become mindless repetitive workers that are a part of a machine. Since there is work division then this creates bureaucratization of organizations. Marx also believed that hierarchy develops not as a way to coordinate work production but to control the means of accumulating capital. Marxists theorists see organizational structures as a similarity of the nation; it is highly influenced by governmental and political structures. He also believed that class stratification and conflict was caused by social relations of productions in a society. The conflict was not related to the individual characteristics of the workers but as a result of their position in the labor system.

Garbage Can model

The Garbage Can Model is from the systemic-anarchic perspective that explain the decision making process of an organization. This theory was developed to explain certain behaviors that contradict the classical theory. In most cases when problems arise in the organization it triggers a response to make decisions, according to the Garbage Can Model, the organization will go through the "garbage" in order to find a solution. This theory uses the term "garbage cans" because the theory states that organizations are able to find solutions and then they are discarded because of a lack of appropriate problems, however different problems may arise and then decision makers have to search through the "garbage" in order to find an appropriate solution. This type of organization can be best understood by viewing choices that are found in various kinds of solutions that have been dumped.

School governance systems

Role of federal government
The primary role of the federal government is to carry out the legal responsibility to protect the right of every citizen to acquire free public education and have an equal opportunity for learning. They must also strive to improve the quality of education by funding research, provide aid to students and understand how to effectively teach so others can learn. The Federal Government does solely fund and administer schools that are established for dependents of military and civilian personnel that are serving overseas. Although the funding is received from the government, the schools are operated under the local school boards. In regards to postsecondary institutions, the Federal government does not exercise any control of the establishment of them nor the standards they maintain. The only is exception is for some academics that would prepare a person for a career officer in the military.

State government's role
The states have their own laws to govern the operation of public schools. These laws guide the policies and requirements for the proper operation of public schools. In most states, a State board of education determines the policies and requirements and carries them out under the leadership of a chief State school officer and professional educators. The laws that govern the membership into the State boards will vary by state. The primary responsibility of the chief State school officer is to distribute funds to local education authorities, overseeing the certifications of teachers, provide training programs for teachers in order to

improve standards, administer State laws, and provide certain services such as advisory services to superintendents and school boards. The States also play a role in deciding the length of the school day and year, graduation requirements, teacher certification standards, transportation, health services and fire protection. They must also oversee that private schools follow the approval process for licensure or accreditation.

States and management
The states have considerable power to help with the success of school-based management by providing support to the schools. Districts should be encouraged by the states to use school-based management as a tool to help students with their performance and the overall schooling conditions. Superintendents and the central office staff need to be well informed that schools will need a great amount of authority and flexibility in order to make this type of management successful for school improvement. In order for a school to properly implement the school-based management process the staff members will need the proper training and research-based information. The states can provide these valuable resources and offer on-site assistance to help schools with the process. If the states can offer these services and the implementation process is successful, then the states can be free of the highly regulated and accountability processes.

Role of local authorities
In each state, except Hawaii, the state is divided into local administrative districts and each district has the responsibility to regulate public schools. The board of education which usually has about five to seven members governs the local districts and operates the public school system through the district staff and the superintendent. The school board and superintendent have the responsibility of preparing the school budget, hiring

personnel, maintaining school buildings, provide the funds for school equipment and supplies and provide transportation for students. They are also responsible for carrying out regulations that govern the operations of schools and they must conform to State law. There are some limitations on the actions of school boards which are regulated by the State legislature or the State education agencies.

School operations management

State level procedures
One of the most primarily important operational functions of the state is to set the minimum standards for all elementary and secondary schools. The state is all responsible for the funding of schools which is primarily done through real property taxes. The states are also responsible for creating laws that ensure the proper operation of public schools and in each state the laws will vary. When the state is involved with the curriculum, it will involve creating guidelines concerning the development and implementation of curricula and ways of assessing student achievement. The state also creates the tests and other performance measures that are required for each academic subject. It is also the responsibility of the state to provide the needed material and resources to local school districts. The state must also decide the graduation requirements in terms of credits and competencies.

District level procedures
The operational procedures at the district level consist mainly of developing policies that concern the curriculum, funding, and teaching. The policies developed through locally elected school board members. Each school district was developed by the state and they must carry out the State laws and regulations that govern the operation of schools. When the district must make decisions about the curriculum, the district can implement any program of study they feel is necessary for their schools, however, it would be to the district's advantage if the program is consistent for each grade level and uniform for each academic subject. The school district should create a mastery core curriculum that will explain the subjects that all schools will offer. A mastery core will also explain the goals and objectives of each subject.

School level procedures
Each school must enact and regulate the operational procedures that made for the school by the school district. However, schools are also responsible for designing and implementing their own operational procedures. It is important that these procedures are expressed clearly to the staff, parents and students. When the school is making curriculum decisions they must first receive the curriculum's goals and objectives from the state and district. The school will also collect the appropriate input from parents and then build a curriculum that is guided by the mastery core. The school should identify their goals and needs and then supplement any classes they feel are necessary to add in order to meet the student's needs. As a team, their will be a decision on the schedule, curriculum integration, and how to align and implement the curriculum.

Education management systems

Participatory government
Participatory government emphasizes the importance of the involvement of everyone involved with the mission and operation of an organization. In regards to education it would translate into the involvement of everyone with an influence of the student's academic achievement. This includes administrators, teachers, parents and students. When everyone is encouraged to participate it makes others feel they

have a voice and their opinion matters. Parents can feel they are helping their child be successful in school and the students can take ownership in their education. Decisions that can be made together are types of fund raising, curriculum ideas and school improvement. Participatory government allows every to have a part and provides a sense of teamwork. There are fewer barriers between administrator and teacher and teacher and parent when everyone is working together.

One of the key elements of participatory management is power. In a school based management system, the decisions are made by team members including the principal, teachers and parents. However, if it were a centralized system the decision making authority is given to members in the central office. The second element of participatory management is how the information is given out and the type of type of information. In a centralized system the information flows from the central office on down to the employees, where as in a participatory management, it is important to have both downward and upward flow of information. The two types of information that are important are information about ideas and information about performance. The type and distribution of awards is the third element because they can cause staff members to become more motivated. The fourth element in participatory management is knowledge and skills.

Site-based management
Site-based management is an approach that makes the individual school responsible for their own curriculum, scheduling, hiring of personnel and budget. This approach allows for more flexibility in deciding what instructional program is best in meeting the individual needs of the students. However, the disadvantage of using this model is often

times individuals can feel confused about what their role and responsibility is. A power struggle can also develop between administrators, teachers and parents. The decision making process lies in the hands of administrators and teachers. This allows teacher to feel more empowered and that their opinions are valued. This approach also allows for more group discussion about decisions regarding the school and for a consensus resolution. A majority vote is usually the basis for decisions.

School-based management
When a school system decides to implement school-based management in the schools there is a major impact on all the roles of the stakeholders. The superintendents are needed to ensure proper implementation of the approach. They have the responsibility to communicate and explain what school-management is to the community and why it is effective. They also are in the role to be supportive of the different approaches individuals may have to school improvement. A principal's role changes the most because they are now looked at as the leader and chief executive. They now have the role of creating programs for
their school instead of enforcing policies that have already been made. Principals have an increased authority and accountability. Teachers are also affected by school-based management. The most important change is they now have a voice in the decision making process instead of having to follow policies that have already been made for them.

School districts and management. Schools will not be successful in a school-based management if they do not have the support of the school district. School districts can help with the success if they clearly express to all stakeholders what it means to have a school-based management and why it is desirable to have this type of organizational structure. Stakeholders should also be informed when this process will take place and how long it will take to fully implement it. Districts can also help by assessing a school's needs and provide the resources to them in order for the process to be successful. Districts should allow the schools the complete authority they need and encourage them to have a site council that includes a representative from the stakeholders. This site council should be responsible for decision making and carrying out improvement plans.

Principals and school-based management. The district will usually specify to some degree to the schools how a school-based management system should function; however, the principal will have a strong influence over the operation. The principal can help make the implementation process more successful if they help the staff and parents understand why there is going to be a change to this type of management and emphasize that is for the improvement of the student's achievement. Principals need to highly educate themselves on this type of management so they are able to answer all questions that teachers and parents may have. Principals should also emphasize that this will be a way to make decisions as a group and all members will have a voice, however the complete implementation process can take up to five years.

Henri Fayol's management principles

Henri Fayol's first principle of management is division of work. He stated that repetition of the same activity will increase output because the person performing will increase their speed. Therefore, the work should be divided according to skill and who can perform that skill the best. The next principle is authority and responsibility. He stated an individual with authority has the right to give orders and expect obedience, however, with this authority comes with great responsibility. Another principle is discipline, which is needed for an organization to run smoothly. Unity of command is also important as well as unity of direction. Each organization must have common goals and be able to follow orders. Fayol's next principle is subordination of interests to the general interest, meaning an individual's interest should be focused on the success of the organization. Fayol's other principles are remuneration of personnel, centralization, line of authority, order, equity, stability of tenure of personnel, initiative and esprit de corps.

Administrator/Manager overlapping duties

An administrator may have to play a role that goes beyond of just the typical duties of an administrator; many times they must act as the manager of the school. When an administrator is making management decisions the goal is to enhance teaching and learning and at the same time remembering what the mission of the school is. Administrators who play the role as manager know how to initiate action that support the school's goals and at the same time demonstrate responsive behavior. Many times these management decisions consist of hiring personnel, maintaining or discontinuing a certain program. An administrator who acts as a manager plans and coordinates activities that help achieve the school's goals. They must make decisions that help and support their staff members.

Group dynamics

Group size
It is best to keep the group size to a smaller number because the more members there are the less comfortable it might become for others. Larger groups often cause the members to feel less

intimate with each other and there will be a decline in the frequency of interaction. Another issue that may come up with larger groups is that the more members there are there is an increase of people with the same interests, dedication and sentiments. If this is the case, then the administrator may have the problem of groups forming within the group. An administrator should find the balance of forming groups with both common and diverse backgrounds and interests. Finding a balance can be difficult because if there is a group with common interests then there is a good chance they will want to work with each other and be cooperative. If there is too much in common then the thoughts and ideas will be the same.

Role behavior in a group

Each individual is different and may exhibit different behaviors in a group. Some work well in groups and others work better by themselves. An administrator may find it difficult to have everyone's participation in a group, especially if they were brought to the group by being told that must participate rather than volunteering for the group. It is very important that the administrator makes sure everyone feels valued and that their opinion matters. In order to receive everyone's full participation it may be necessary to assign roles. Each person has a specific job and it is their responsibility to make sure that job is fulfilled. It may be necessary to change roles every so often, because the individuals who like to work in groups may always take an active role while others may fall back and get lost in the group. Which ever method is done, it is the administrator's responsibility to ensure everyone feels valued and their opinion is needed for the cohesiveness of the group.

Group problems

When an administrator becomes the leader of the group, he or she needs to be aware of the problems that may occur. Many times no problems occur and the goal of the group can be achieved quickly. However, in some cases there are problems. One problem is that many times an individual will have no interest being apart of a group do not understand why they are a part of a group and therefore not have the commitment like the others. Therefore, communication as to why this group has formed and what the goal is should be a top priority. Another problem that may occur is a group that is unable to be productive and only create conflict. It is important that the administrator create a respectful and productive environment. An administrator might also find it difficult to keep the groups attention on the task at hand.

Sources of social conflict

Social conflict occurs when certain groups of the school community are at odds with one another. Poor communication is often the leading cause of conflict. Teachers can develop negative attitudes and be unwilling to strive and achieve the school goals if they do not feel encouraged or appreciated. That is why it is so important for administrators to give feedback and express their appreciation for their teachers. If the school has an organizational structure where the administrator makes all the decisions and the staff's opinions do not matter, there will be an increase in conflict. Schools where teachers feel empowered and there are group decision makers will experience conflict, however they will be minor. Other factors, such as personality and different values can cause conflict; however, they cannot be changed only managed appropriately. Conflict can also be caused by limited resources; therefore, it is the administrator's responsibility to ensure the resources that are available are given out fairly.

Managing programs and services

Pupil personnel service

Administrators must maintain the organizational and operational features of the school's programs and services. One of these services is the pupil personnel service. It is defined in the Elementary and Secondary Education Act (ESEA, as reauthorized under the No Child Left Behind Act, Sec. 9101, paragraph 36) as "school counselors, school social workers, school psychologists, and other qualified professional personnel involved in providing assessment, diagnosis, counseling, educational, therapeutic, and other necessary services." These staff members work together in order to help assist with any student that may have a learning disability or any other issue that may hinder their learning capabilities. The goal is to work together to ensure that every student is given the opportunity to reach their full academic potential. The focus is to prevent or have intervention activities developed for the individual student that helps them succeed in school.

Student activities

One of the duties of an administrator is overseeing the operational features of the school, including student activities. It is important for students to be able to participate in programs that are of their interest. A student who is involved in something they enjoy will more likely have confidence in themselves and a higher self esteem. Many of the programs can include student council, choir, cheerleading, band and many others. Administrators must also handle the ancillary services, which can take up a lot of the administrator's time. Many school districts are looking toward outsourcing ancillary services and have found this allows administrators to focus more of their time on educational responsibilities. Administrators need to be aware of any rules or regulations against outsourcing before moving ahead with it.

Human resource management

Norms

Norms can be described as unwritten rules that state what others believe should and should be done and they can help regulate and control behavior. It is important for administrators to remember that norms cannot be pushed onto a group and force that group to believe in them. Each person that comes to work at a school already has values of their own that they strongly believe in. If an administrator wants an effective organizational culture then it is important that he or she hires staff with similar norms and values that the administrator feels are needed for an effective school. If a staff member feels they are in an environment where their values beliefs are shared then their work performance will be higher and they will have more job satisfaction. If the school changes its focus then it is a result of changes in staff that change the values of the school.

Expectations. The expectations of an organization are developed based on what the norms are of the school. It is important that administrators are aware of the expectations of the school. It is impossible for an administrator to live up to every expectation from every staff member; however it is important for the administrator to be aware of is expected from them in order to fully understand the school culture. It is also important that the merit of these expectations be evaluated before they are met. The expectations may be too unrealistic to the school goals and to its mission. If expectations are too high this could cause a conflict with the organization, however, if they are too low then others may not be reaching their full potential. This will only

Copyright © Mometrix Media. You have been licensed one copy of this document for personal use only. Any other reproduction or redistribution is strictly prohibited. All rights reserved.

have a negative on the students and their academic potential.

Clear job descriptions
If an administrator wants to prevent or reduce the likelihood of conflict, then it is crucial that clear job descriptions are developed for every position in an organization. When individuals understand what is expected of them and what their responsibilities are they are less likely to fail meeting the expectations of others. In many situations individuals who do not know their responsibilities may assume a role of another and may be viewed as going beyond what is expected of them. It would be best if the administrator review the job descriptions and ensure they have clear descriptions. It would also be helpful to review it with the person who occupies that position and with someone who has expectations of that position. This would help gain full commitment to the role. The job description should also be communicated periodically to the person who holds the position.

Staff personnel
An administrator has a vital role in the organizational and operational process of hiring staff personnel. When hiring personnel it is important that the administrator remember their role as the culture developer. An administrator has the ability to change the school's culture with every hire of a new person. They should hire individuals who share the common goals and interests of the school. Administrators also play a role in how to recruit personnel; they must choose the appropriate approach to recruitment, whether it is a job fair or visiting college campuses. Another crucial decision an administrator must make is what the appropriate placement of this new hire is. Administrators must decide in what area or grade level the new staff member will new be most beneficial to the students and school. Then, administrators must

continue with the appropriate monitoring process to ensure the new staff member is equipped with the necessary resources to help the school achieve its goals.

Personnel selections. It is crucial that an administrator select appropriate personnel in order to reduce the amount of role conflict. When an individual interviews for a position, they must be told what is expected of them and the type of person it takes to fulfill that position. Once this has been done, then the hiring committee can chose from a variety of selection processes. An administrator can receive important insight information during the selection process, especially from individuals who hold certain expectations about that position, for example, teachers. Once a person has been hired, their responsibilities and expectations should be clearly expressed to them and may need to be expressed periodically. Feedback may need to be given to that person in order for them to ensure the quality of their job performance.

Human resource administration policies and procedures

National associations
Most national associations are non-profit membership organizations that represent their member's interests before the government. Other responsibilities of an association are assisting their members with certain services and they may also help regulate certain standards that are in their area of interest and jurisdiction. Although associations are non-governmental organizations, they can have a powerful influence in national policymaking and are sometimes consulted by the government in regards to the association's area of expertise. Many teachers' unions can provide teachers with services such as legal council and provide teachers a voice where they believe reform is needed. If a

teacher feels there are situations where it hinders their ability to teach and the district has not made an effort to improve it, a teacher can go to their union and they can put pressure on individuals to fix the situation.

Affirmative action

Affirmative action is a policy that tries to redress past discrimination by taking measures to ensure there is an equal opportunity for employment regardless of race, gender, age, ethnicity or disabilities. The goal is to counteract past discriminations that were targeted toward certain demographic groups. Many opponents to affirmative action state that it may increase the racial tension instead of settling it down. Many also say that in cases such as college admissions it hurts those it intends to help by causing a mismatch effect, meaning a minority student that is less qualified may be admitted rather than someone who is well qualified. It is an administrator's responsibility to be up to date on the affirmative action policies and understand the importance of it when it pertains to their school.

Collective bargaining

Collective bargaining is an agreement between an employer and the employee usually involving the employee's labor union. The agreement will usually state what terms have been agreed upon, which usually will include wages, hours worked, benefits and other employment issues. A collective bargaining agreement cannot address every issue that might arise, however there can be an unwritten agreement about how conflict will be resolved, external law and customs of the school. Although a wide range of topics can be agreed upon, the federal and state laws limit it to some degree. The agreement cannot violate any civil rights or reduce safety standards that are clearly stated under the Occupational Safety and Health Act. There is not a requirement

that states the employer and union must reach an agreement, however, there should be bargaining done in good faith over certain subjects.

Managing facilities and auxillary services

School safety and security

Every teacher and student has the right to come to school and know their safety and security will not be jeopardized. A student cannot be expected to learn and teacher cannot be expected to teacher if they feel their safety is in danger. As an administrator, it is their responsibility to ensure that every measure has been taken to ensure that every student and teacher feels safe. One way to create a positive school culture is to encourage students and teachers to behave in ways that help to create a safe and orderly environment. Administrators can also establish a zero tolerance policy in regards to violence. This policy establishes the consequences of violent behavior and they are strongly expressed ahead of time to every student and there will be absolutely zero tolerance of that kind of behavior.

Many schools have implemented metal detectors, however, that only prevents weapons from being brought in and it does not prevent violence within the school walls. One way an administrator can help with school violence is implementing school violence prevention programs. These types of programs help students develop skills for handling conflict. These skills are built around how to avoid conflict, how to respond appropriately once conflict has begun, and how to remove themselves from conflict situations if the other person's behavior makes it impossible to resolve the issue. Another way an administrator can help with school violence is through mediation. Students can learn beneficial life skills when using the mediation approach. These violence prevention training programs can be more beneficial than criminal enforcement techniques.

If an administrator is looking for resources to help in violence prevention, the internet can provide extremely important information. There are several sources of information that discuss what leads to school violence and what is the most effective way of preventing it. Administrators can find journals that discuss the latest research on the early warning signs and how to develop a useful prevention plan. Another resourceful piece of information is the Safeguarding Our Children: An Action Guide which provides information on how schools can use a model that stresses, prevention, early intervention, and services for children with behavioral and emotional needs. An effective administrator must always stay informed and educated about the latest research that can help benefit their school.

Plant operation and maintenance

The purpose of utilizing the plant operation and maintenance is to provide the school building with a service that will ensure a clean, safe, comfortable and appealing environment. The individuals who take part in the plant operation and maintenance should be qualified and given efficient and effective tools and materials in order to keep the building in the condition it should be in to create an effective learning environment. This division provides proper training for the staff, how to inspect the building and helps to maintain an inventory of cleaning supplies. It is important that the staff members in charge of plant operations and maintenance are given the proper funds for supplies, equipment and materials needed for repairs and with the maintaining of cleaning equipment.

Fiscal and program resource management

Centralized budget

In a centralized budget system, the school district pays the bills, collects revenues, distributes resources to the schools as needed and ensures that all individuals are given an equal portion of revenues. The risks are low with a centralized budget, however, so are the rewards. A school can not control their own fortune and individuals will can benefit or not according to the economic situation at a certain time. This type of budget process does not allow for individuals to be creative and enhance an individual's entrepreneurial spirit. Although this type of budget distributes the revenues equally so that it does not cause conflict between the schools, it does not eliminate the possibility of conflict within the budget department as to how much funding each school will get.

Decentralized budget

In a decentralized budget system each school pays for its own expenses and keeps most of the revenue it generates, giving the school more financial responsibility and accountability. This allows for more freedom to be creative with ways on how to earn revenue and how the funds will be given. This type of budget process can have high risk; there is no back up from the district if the money runs out. However, the potential growth is much higher than a centralized budget system. There is no limit on how much money one school can earn, this in return can motivate the staff members, teachers, parents and students to generate more funds for the school. Administrators must ensure that the strategic planning for spending funds aligns with the school's goals and the mission.

Site-based budgeting

Site-based budgeting moves authority and resources away from district power and places the responsibility on the local school. When districts choose to use site-based budgeting the school has the authority to determine staffing levels that are within contract, choose vendors and service providers. They also have the freedom to make purchases without filing special paperwork or ask for permission. When schools use site-based budgeting, the decision making process is left in the hands of the administrator, teachers and at times communities leaders. This type of approach allows more flexibility within the school and can build a culture of trust among administrators, staff, parents and students. This approach can also increase student achievement because the schools can make important decisions regarding the students because they know the needs of the students.

Zero-based budgeting

Zero-based budgeting is an approach to budgeting that is based on the idea that all activities will be examined before they are included in the budget, regardless if they were in the budget the year before. When using a zero-based budgeting process it is important that the administrator remember what the mission and goals are of the school when beginning to make the budget. The administrator will have to examine each program and activity that was in the budget last year and determine if those programs and activities are needed to help achieve student success. There may have to be a time when the administrator will need to rank the importance and need of each program. Once the administrator has determined which programs will be added to the budget, then a decision needs to be made on how to allocate resources to each one.

Practice Test

Practice Questions

1. Collegial relationships among faculty and staff members will help ensure effective teaching, learning, and collaboration. As principal, which of the following will foster positive relationships and help promote a unified school vision?
   a. Surveying faculty and staff members to elicit their opinions on a range of topics at the first faculty meeting of each quarter or semester.
   b. Keeping an "open door policy" one or two days per week to allow faculty members the opportunity to share insights and opinions.
   c. Surveying faculty and staff at each and every faculty meeting while also keeping a permanent "open door policy."
   d. Not eliciting opinions of faculty and staff before new program implementation.

2. Parents and caregivers are valuable assets to educational campuses and should be engaged in the education of their children. As principal, which of the following will provide a variety of opportunities to engage parents?
   a. Send flyers home at the start of each quarter or semester announcing different school events.
   b. Invite parents to school frequently to provide them with a host of meaningful volunteer opportunities that use their suggestions, as well as opportunities to visit classrooms.
   c. Attend one PTO or PTA meeting every few months.
   d. Provide parents with the chance to voice their opinions and suggestions.

3. At a high school special education eligibility meeting, a prior incident involving alcohol is discussed by the student's mother. The parent demands to know what consequences were given to the other students. What is the proper response from the principal?
   a. To tell the parent what consequences were given to all students involved.
   b. To change the topic without answering her question.
   c. To remind the parent what consequences were given to her child only, and to remind her that the purpose of the meeting is to determine special education eligibility, not to discuss breaches of conduct.
   d. To ask her what she thinks the punishment should have been.

4. The principal is considering the adoption of podcasts in the foreign language curriculum. What are some of the appropriate steps the principal should take before deciding to purchase the required curriculum and ancillary materials?
   a. Poll the faculty as a whole to elicit their opinions on the idea.
   b. Survey the foreign language department to secure their opinions. Secondly, examine the economic trends that would warrant such a purchase. Finally, use current research in curriculum design to ensure podcasts would effectively meet the needs of all students.
   c. Discuss the idea with the district's foreign language coordinator and allow the coordinator to make the decision.
   d. Poll the students to gauge their interest level in participating in a course that uses such a curriculum.

5. A high school principal is determining scheduling and staffing needs for the coming school year. In order to effectively meet the needs of all students, the principal should create the schedule based on:
   a. The principal's own agenda and preferences.
   b. The number of students and faculty per grade level.
   c. The equitable allotment of resources based on intense analysis of instructional needs.
   d. Directives issued from central office or other high school principals.

6. An effective faculty or staff meeting has which of the following components:
   a. an "open forum" orientation where staff members are free to choose the topics for discussion.
   b. A rigid, agenda-based meeting that essentially consists of administrators lecturing and advising teachers of important upcoming dates and events.
   c. A forum in which the principal addresses faculty concerns, discusses topics of interest, and provides meaningful professional development on a range of issues and content areas.
   d. Infrequent meetings without structured agendas.

7. The principal of Smith Middle School would like to adopt a new set of manipulatives for the math curriculum. In order to effectively implement such a change, she will:
   a. Deliver a set of manipulatives to each math teacher with an instruction manual.
   b. Hold an in-service day to allow teachers the chance to familiarize themselves with the new ancillary material.
   c. Give teachers the opportunity to attend the county-wide training over a two-day period where they can learn from teachers who already use the manipulatives.
   d. Send all math teachers to the national manipulative training workshop for five days.

8. The principal of Jones Middle School is having a safety issue in the bus lanes during dismissal. He is understaffed at the end of the day due to sports practice and other extracurricular activities. Also, one of his assistant principals is ineffective and is constantly absent from school. He really needs one more adult to monitor students boarding the bus. To best apply his problem-solving skills, he will:
   a. ask a first year teacher who already has a cafeteria duty to help him in the bus lanes.
   b. Ask the basketball coach to start practice ten minutes later so the coach can help out in the bus lanes.
   c. Dismiss students on a staggered time basis so there are not as many in the bus lanes at one time.
   d. Discuss absenteeism with his assistant principal and devise a collaborative plan to change the AP's behaviors.

9. It has come to the attention of the principal of Holmes Elementary School that several faculty members have been stealing items from the supply closet. What are the appropriate steps for the principal to take?
   a. Immediately report the teachers to the county offices for consequences.
   b. Lock the supply cabinet and issue keys only to the administrative assistants in the building.
   c. First confirm that the teachers are indeed taking supplies, and if the information is correct, devise a plan that will allow teachers to "order" supplies from the closet on a weekly or monthly basis. Also, address the bigger issue of teachers stealing items from their employers for non-work use.
   d. Ask the custodians to monitor the supply closet.

10. Lately there has been a problem with teens putting graffiti on external school walls. In order to address the issue, the principal should:
   a. ask the local police to monitor or stake out the school daily.
   b. Clean off the graffiti the same day it is written; appoint a volunteer committee comprised of students and faculty to help keep the school clean; dole out appropriate punishments to the students caught writing the graffiti; address the larger issue of defacing school property at grade-level meetings.
   c. Stake out the school himself/herself.
   d. Allow student volunteers to attempt to catch the graffiti-writers in the act.

11. An intruder enters a school building. Luckily, no one is hurt or injured and the intruder is captured by police. The principal was able to ensure no injuries or casualties in the crisis because he prepared by:
   a. Verbally telling staff and students how to respond in a crisis.
   b. Having a written crisis plan and safe evacuation route for all classrooms in the building and holding monthly crisis drills in which students and staff practice safe evacuation or protection for a variety of potential crises.
   c. Reminding the staff at faculty meeting of the appropriate response to crises.
   d. Posting the evacuation or protection plans on the school walls.

Questions 12 to 20 pertain to the following scenario:
   Ms. Rose has just been appointed as the new principal of Howard Middle School. Upon reviewing the discipline referrals, she notices a large discrepancy in the number of disciplinary actions taken in different groups of students. In order to figure out the discrepancy, Ms. Rose observes classrooms and surveys teachers, students, and parents.

12. After observing a cross-section of classrooms at Howard Middle School, Ms. Rose realizes that the needs of all students are not being met. She draws this conclusion based on her observation that:
   a. Many students have been placed in certain classes based on their socio-economic status (SES), not their actual learning ability.
   b. Most students complain when not seated with their friends.
   c. There are too many students in one classroom.
   d. Students are reluctant to do their homework.

13. Specifically, Ms. Rose notes that many athletes are given preferential treatment, leading to a disgruntled student population of non-athletes. Which of the following steps should she take to ensure fair and equitable treatment for all students?
   a. Collaboratively write a new conduct policy to ensure equal treatment and implementation.
   b. Suggest to the teachers that they not treat athletes differently.
   c. Support teachers when they refer students for disciplinary action.
   d. Examine the current discipline policy to find inconsistencies.

14. During her observations, Ms. Rose also notes that some discipline policies need revision. Which of the following is most indicative of this need for revision?
   a. There is no meaningful consequence for students who do not serve detentions, which leads to further discipline referrals.
   b. Students are expected to apologize for egregious behavior.
   c. Students who are caught vandalizing the school are charged with repairing the vandalism as part of their consequence.
   d. Students serving after-school and Saturday detentions often act as custodians.

15. Over the past three years, there has been a thirty percent rise in the number of immigrant students. How can Ms. Rose best determine if the needs of these students are being met?
   a. By examining the number of students who participate in extracurricular activities such as drama, band, and so forth.
   b. By examining the number of immigrant students in special education.
   c. By examining the number of students who participate in sports.
   d. By examining the attrition rate of all students.

16. Additionally, what is another factor Ms. Rose should examine to see if all students' needs are being met?
   a. The number of parents who attend Parents' Night or conferences.
   b. The number of these students in the English for Speakers of Other Languages (ESOL) program.
   c. The number of teachers who attend professional development programs.
   d. The number of paraprofessionals placed in each room.

17. After reviewing the data and observing classrooms, Ms. Rose is also concerned with the number of students who are missing valuable instructional time. Which of the following data would she use to support her claim?
   a. The number of students who visit the school nurse for non-emergency purposes.
   b. The number of students who participate in sports programs.
   c. The number of students who are pulled out for ESOL or special education testing.
   d. The number of students who receive weekly enrichment in music or art.

18. What is a second piece of data that Ms. Rose would use to support her claim that students are missing valuable instructional time?
   a. The number of students on student council.
   b. The number of students who arrive late or leave early.
   c. The number of students involved in the peer tutoring program.
   d. The number of students in the chorus or band.

19. During her investigation of discipline referrals, Ms. Rose discovers that many students who are receiving disciplinary action are age-inappropriate for their grade levels. Which of the following would *best* serve as an intervention program to combat retention?
   a. Mandatory after-school mentoring and tutoring program with courses based on student weaknesses.
   b. Placement in remedial-level classes.
   c. Participation in a homework help line.
   d. Extra help sessions with teachers.

20. What is a second intervention program that Ms. Rose should offer to *best* help students who are age-inappropriate for their grade level?
   a. after-school job placement.
   b. Volunteering in the community.
   c. Counseling or coaching to ensure grade promotion requirements.
   d. Encouraging students to participate in sports.

Question 21 pertains to the following scenario:
   *a*fter conducting her study of the discipline referral system at Howard Middle School, Ms. Rose hosts a parent night to communicate the future changes of the discipline system with parents.

21. During the meeting, many parents agree with intervention programs being put into place, but many are unsure about their role in the new policies. What would be the *best* idea for Ms. Rose suggest to parents?
   a. To drop off and pick up students from school.
   b. To attend parent conferences.
   c. To frequently communicate with teachers and to support student attendance at mentoring sessions.
   d. To occasionally call the school to check in on student progress.

Questions 22 and 23 pertain to the following scenario:
   Ms. Rose also decides to address the issue of discipline at the next faculty meeting. She brings with her the responses from the parent night.

22. The teachers agree generally with all the suggestions made by Ms. Rose and the parents, but question the implementation of the mentoring program. They are concerned with being asked to perform tasks on a volunteer basis and worry that there will not be enough staff to effectively run the program and help the students. What should Ms. Rose do to create teacher buy-in?
   a. Support faculty discussion about the program and allow them to make suggestions.
   b. Survey staff to cull their ideas on how to create a successful program; use their ideas to run the program.
   c. Have teachers contact parents to form solid relationships between home and school.
   d. Ask for parent volunteers to run the program.

23. Some months later, Ms. Rose reads the PTA newsletter, in which there is a negative editorial about some of the changes she has made at Howard Middle School. What action should Ms. Rose take to combat negative press?
   a. Write a rebuttal editorial detailing all the positive changes in the school and reiterating the school's vision.
   b. Encourage staff to write similar rebuttal editorials.
   c. Encourage supportive parents to write similar rebuttal editorials.
   d. Invite the PTA president, as well as other members of the press, to tour the school in order to share the mission and vision with them and to provide evidence of positive change and student success.

Questions 24 to 30 pertain to the following scenario:

Mr. Jones has been the principal at Norton High School for the past five years. While he believes that the faculty and staff are highly effective, he wants to change the current schedule of semesters to trimesters in order to give students more opportunities for electives and college-placement courses. He performs a site visit at a school that has a similar trimester schedule, and proposes the idea to the school improvement committee.

24. What data should Mr. Jones *first* examine to determine whether his idea will meet the needs of all students?
   a. The graduation rate of Norton High School.
   b. The retention rate among the freshman class.
   c. The percentage of Norton High School students who attend college.
   d. The percentage of Norton High School students who graduate from college.

25. What data should Mr. Jones examine *next* in order to determine whether his idea will meet the needs of all students?
   a. Disaggregated data by gender, race, etc. of students who graduate from Norton High School.
   b. The percentage of students who attend trade or vocational schools after high school graduation.
   c. The percentage of students who attend state universities.
   d. The percentage of students who participate in sports.

26. Once he has determined potential feasibility, what is the *first* step that Mr. Jones should take to suggest this change to the school improvement committee?
   a. announce the proposed change and present a formal proposal.
   b. Discuss the site visit with committee members and poll their willingness to proceed with the feasibility study; anticipate questions and assuage their fears.
   c. Distribute a new schedule and teaching duties based on the new trimester schedule.
   d. Ask which teachers would like to participate in a site visit as well.

27. During the school improvement meeting, most of the teachers are willing to investigate the idea of trimesters and are also willing to perform a feasibility study. Yet a few teachers adamantly refuse to consider the proposal and have not heard all the background information. What is Mr. Jones's best choice to combat the negative attitudes of those few teachers?
   a. Ignore them and proceed by focusing on the majority of teachers in the meeting.
   b. Discuss their negative responses with them.
   c. Ask them to share their own ideas and give them tasks that speak to their strengths.
   d. Appoint them as heads of the school improvement committee.

28. Mr. Jones also plans to enlist the help of the community in his endeavor to change the schedule. Which of the following would *best* help him get community members on board?
   a. Survey community members to see which courses they feel should be offered.
   b. Allow them to tour the school to see what is currently happening in a typical school day.
   c. Offer them monetary incentives to support the trimester plan.
   d. Ask community members to donate money to the school.

29. How else can Mr. Jones involve community members in the process?
   a. ask them to serve on the school improvement committee.
   b. Create a cooperative school-to-work program in which students could receive credit for "apprenticeships" or working at community businesses.
   c. Ask them to coach sports teams or help out in music and art programs.
   d. Ask them to run field trips to different educational locations.

30. Let us assume that several months have passed and the faculty now supports the adoption of the new trimester schedule. What is the *best* way for Mr. Jones and the faculty to select the new course offerings?
   a. allow parents to suggest course offerings.
   b. Allow teachers to choose what they prefer to teach.
   c. Incorporate curriculum that is based on current research, emerging issues, and economic trends.
   d. Allow students to suggest course offerings.

Questions 31 to 35 pertain to the following scenario:
   *a*s the principal of Hammond High School, Ms. Smith regularly holds office hours for staff to express suggestions and concerns. The following are several scenarios with which she was presented:

31. Mr. Lawrence, a veteran teacher, approaches Ms. Smith regarding a stalemate in his department. Several teachers wish to use collaborative and standardized assessments, yet he feels that individual teachers should be able to assess students based on their individual needs. What can Ms. Smith do to *best* help resolve this conflict?
   a. Tell Mr. Lawrence that majority rules and he should do as the other teachers ask.
   b. Ask the department coordinator to address the issue.
   c. Listen to both sides of the argument and come to a collaborative decision or compromise regarding assessments.
   d. Tell the other teachers to follow Mr. Lawrence's directive.

32. Ms. Jones, a first-year teacher, comes to Ms. Smith's office regarding a conversation between herself, her department coordinator, and a parent. The parent was upset because of one of Ms. Jones' grading practices. The department coordinator told the parent that Ms. Jones was in the wrong and apologized for her actions. However, Ms. Jones is distressed because her grading practices follow school guidelines and the coordinator spoke to the parent behind her back. How should Ms. Smith *best* resolve this issue?
   a. Tell Ms. Jones that her grading practices are within guidelines and for her not to worry.
   b. Hold a meeting with the coordinator and review proper leadership responsibilities. Then, hold a meeting with both the coordinator and the teacher to resolve the issue.
   c. Call the parent directly and apologize for the confusion.
   d. Tell Ms. Jones to listen to whatever the coordinator says.

33. The science coordinator tells Ms. Smith that a science teacher is habitually late to work. How can the coordinator and Ms. Smith *best* address the issue?
   a. Put a copy of the teacher's contract in his mailbox with the attendance portions highlighted.
   b. Send a reprimanding email to the teacher.
   c. Tell the coordinator to deal with the issue.
   d. Meet with the teacher to ascertain the reason for tardiness and generate solutions to eliminate the problem.

34. Several parents have filed complaints about a teacher who makes inappropriate statements in class. What is the *best* way for Ms. Smith to address the issue?
   a. Observe the teacher on several unannounced occasions and speak with the teacher regarding appropriate and inappropriate behavior. Meet with the parents to assure them that the situation has been appropriately handled.
   b. Tell the parents that no teacher at Hammond High School would make such comments.
   c. Ask the students if the claims are correct.
   d. Issue a formal warning in writing to the teacher.

35. The fire code states that only a certain percentage of classroom walls can be covered with posters, etc. The custodian approaches Ms. Smith because several teachers refuse to comply with the fire code, despite repeated requests to change the wall coverings. How can Ms. Smith *best* address this issue?
   a. Remove the wall decorations herself.
   b. Have the fire marshal issue a formal citation to the teachers.
   c. Meet privately with the teachers to ensure they comply with the fire code.
   d. Have the custodian remove the wall decorations.

36. Over the past three years, the principal of an elementary school with a diverse socioeconomic population has introduced a new "Character Counts" program. According to the competencies, this initiative measures which responsibility of a principal?
   a. Developing and implementing plans for using technology and information systems.
   b. Implementing strategies to ensure the development of collegial relationships.
   c. Applying skills for building consensus and managing conflict.
   d. Promoting awareness of learning differences, multicultural awareness, gender sensitivity, and ethnic appreciation.

37. The principal and site-based curriculum committee of a high school have decided to offer Advanced Placement classes in foreign language. However, enrollment is low. What could they have done *prior to* making the curriculum change to ensure student interest and involvement?
   a. Surveyed teachers for their opinions.
   b. Surveyed students to gauge their interest.
   c. Performed a feasibility study including interest, budget, and curriculum pieces.
   d. Surveyed parents for their opinions on the course.

38. In reference to question # 37, what is the best way for the principal and committee to now raise enrollment?
   a. Offer incentives to students who enroll in the classes.
   b. Offer seminars and professional development for all stakeholders to ensure that all interested parties have a solid grasp of the course and its benefits.
   c. Penalize students who do not enroll.
   d. Try to get parents to enroll students on their own.

39. The county has issued a new directive that Washington Middle School and High School will be International Baccalaureate schools. The accreditation process takes several years and requires a tremendous amount of collaborative work. The principal has determined that there are enough funds to send five teachers to an out-of-town professional development training. How can the principal select the *best* five teachers from the school to attend the conference?
   a. Send the teachers with the top seniority.
   b. Send the teachers with whom the principal has a close relationship.
   c. Send teachers that represent a cross-section of grade levels and content areas.
   d. Send only the department coordinators.

40. The adoption of the International Baccalaureate program requires a complete mission and vision change. How can the principal most effectively create the new vision?
   a. By asking teachers to accept his new vision.
   b. By creating a forum in which teachers and other stakeholders can voice opinions and include their ideas in the new vision.
   c. By asking the parents or PTA to create the new mission statement or vision.
   d. By asking students to create the new mission statement or vision.

41. The International Baccalaureate program requires block scheduling, but no teacher in the building has ever taught in a block scheduling situation. How can the principal help the teachers acquire the skill set necessary to teach in a block scheduling environment?
   a. Have them read instructional articles on implementing block scheduling.
   b. Have them perform site visits to other schools that effectively use block scheduling.
   c. Send one teacher to professional development and have that teacher report back to the entire faculty.
   d. Send a few teachers to a day-long workshop and have them report back to the entire faculty.

Questions 42 and 43 pertain to the following graph:

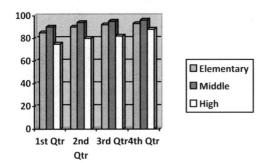

42. The above bar graph shows overall student averages for elementary, middle and high school students in a high-functioning district. There is an obvious drop in scores when the students reach high school. What could be one reason for this change?
    a. The elementary and middle programs are too easy.
    b. There is no scope and sequence among all grade-level curriculums.
    c. The high school programs are too difficult.
    d. The students lose interest in school as they get older.

43. Conversely, there is a rise in scores from elementary to middle school. What could be one reason for this change?
    a. Lower-performing students attend a different middle school.
    b. Students become more interested in school as they get older.
    c. The teachers in middle school use strategies that meet the needs of all students and secure student achievement.
    d. The elementary school teachers have prepared the students for middle school.

Questions 44 to 52 pertain to the following scenario:
> Due to re-districting, two elementary schools are merging. Both are very small, yet one is homogenous while the other has quite a diverse student and faculty population. Mr. Phillips has just been named principal of the new school, and has begun to address the concerns of the stakeholders.

44. The faculty of the homogenous school is concerned about teaching a diverse population. What can Mr. Phillips do to *best* assuage their fears?
    a. Visit other exemplary diverse schools and learn from the new teachers joining the staff.
    b. Watch a training video on teaching diverse populations.
    c. Instruct them to use the same pedagogical methods as usual.
    d. Send them to professional development programs.

45. Several teachers will have to be displaced due to space and faculty allotment issues. How can Mr. Phillips most effectively select teachers to be displaced?
    a. By only keeping his favorite teachers.
    b. By making the selections based on seniority.
    c. By displacing ineffective teachers.
    d. By managing the human resources according to district policies and campus priorities.

46. Mr. Phillips communicates his decision about teacher placement to individual teachers and makes general announcements to the faculty as a whole. The purpose of this open communication is to:
    a. Maintain an atmosphere of respect regarding the decision-making process.
    b. Make his viewpoint known.
    c. Impress the teachers.
    d. Allow the teachers an opportunity to express their opinions.

47. Regarding curricular changes in the new school, how can Mr. Phillips promote a feeling of stakeholder ownership?
    a. By informing all the stakeholders of the decisions after they are made.
    b. By asking teachers first, then having the teachers communicate the decisions to the remaining groups.
    c. Surveying all stakeholders and active parties at special curriculum meetings and using their suggestions.
    d. By making the final decisions seem like someone else's idea.

48. In terms of the physical plant, how can Mr. Phillips most effectively use the space in the new building?
    a. By allowing teachers to select their own rooms.
    b. By following fire and civic codes as well as district policies to ensure student safety.
    c. By giving classroom priority to first-year teachers.
    d. By giving classroom priority to senior or veteran teachers.

49. Mr. Phillips hosts a faculty picnic to facilitate the merge and to help teachers get to know each other. Also, this provides him with an opportunity to:
    a. Identify the negative teachers.
    b. Understand and appreciate his faculty for their talents.
    c. Showcase his talents.
    d. Demonstrate his willingness to host social functions.

50. At the faculty picnic, Mr. Phillips is introduced to an assistant principal who was also a candidate for the principal position. The AP is quite negative and holds a grudge because he was not selected as principal. How can Mr. Phillips most effectively build a working relationship with this AP?
    a. By allowing the AP to demonstrate his talents and validating his ideas and skills.
    b. By keeping a very formal distance and performing in a top-down manner.
    c. By asking around for background information on the AP.
    d. By delegating more responsibility to the AP.

51. Several parents contact Mr. Phillips to share their concerns regarding the schools' merger. Most notably, they are worried about combining two PTAs and creating an association with representation for both schools. What can Mr. Phillips do to help address parental concerns and eliminate this issue?
    a. allow one PTA to fully absorb the other.
    b. Hold a meeting with the two current PTA presidents and allow them to brainstorm ideas.
    c. Disband both PTAs and start from scratch.
    d. Allow all current PTA members to make the final decision.

52. A prominent community member wrote an editorial for the local paper expressing his dissatisfaction with the district combining the two elementary schools, even though he had previously supported the endeavor. How can Mr. Phillips prevent future negative press?
    a. By badmouthing the newspaper and refusing to order a subscription.
    b. By inviting the community member to tour the school.
    c. By encouraging others to cancel their subscriptions to the paper.
    d. By issuing his own editorial as a rebuttal.

53. A principal has adopted an advisement program to help struggling students with academic and social issues. She observes that three teachers on the faculty to not implement the program correctly. How can she *best* address this issue?
    a. By emailing the entire staff and demanding that they follow the advisement program.
    b. By emailing the three teachers and asking them to properly follow the program.
    c. By visiting each of the three teachers personally and addressing any concerns they have; after those concerns are collaboratively addressed, informing the teachers that part of their job requirement is to follow the advisement program.
    d. By sending the assistant principal to deal with the issue.

54. Several high school teachers do not follow the dress code and dress inappropriately for the work place. What should the principal do to *best* solve this problem?
    a. Issue a written warning to each teacher.
    b. Place a copy of the contract with the dress code highlighted in each teacher's mailbox.
    c. Email the entire staff to remind them of the proper dress code.
    d. Speak personally with each teacher who is not observing the dress code; follow up with a written warning and further steps if no change is made.

55. A middle school principal wants to create a peer tutoring program. What is the most effective way to create faculty buy-in and interest?
    a. asking for input from the faculty on how to create such a program.
    b. Offering money to the adviser.
    c. After eliciting feedback and using it, compensating the program adviser with a small stipend.
    d. Allowing the students to create the policies and practices for the program.

56. A high school English teacher is issued a formal warning for reading inappropriate materials in class. During a routine classroom observation, the principal notices an age-inappropriate book on the book shelf. What is the *first* action the principal should take?
    a. Inform the police.
    b. Examine the district's personnel and human resources policies and act accordingly.
    c. Fire the teacher immediately.
    d. Inform the media of the infraction.

57. An elementary school bus driver leaves a kindergarten student on the bus while she runs into the grocery store. The parent first calls the school principal to complain. What is the *first* thing the principal should do?
   a. Suspend the bus driver.
   b. Confirm that the child is not injured or harmed in any way.
   c. Call the bus company.
   d. Call the police.

58. A high school student is accused by a teacher of a stealing a cell phone from the classroom. How can the principal *best* handle the issue?
   a. Listen to both sides of the story to ascertain what, in fact, happened.
   b. Immediately take the teacher's word.
   c. Immediately take the student's word.
   d. Suspend the student for five days' out-of-school suspension.

59. A middle school principal observes a teacher with several years' experience. She notes that the teacher has several areas for improvement, most notably that students are not engaged in the learning process. When the principal meets with the teacher, the teacher says he does not feel the need to change because no one has told him that before. What is the principal's *best* response?
   a. Insist that the teacher make changes.
   b. Use specific observation data and collaboration to help the teacher make changes.
   c. Write a formal complaint that the teacher is non-compliant.
   d. Ask other teachers to demonstrate good pedagogy.

60. There is an opening for a fifth grade teacher at James Elementary School. The principal interviewed three very similar candidates and must make a decision soon. What criteria should the principal *first* examine to help make his decision on whom to hire?
   a. The teachers' college education
   b. The teachers' salary requirements
   c. The teachers' educational philosophy
   d. The teachers' teaching experience

Question 61 pertains to the following scenario:
   Mr. Ross has been appointed principal of Colonel High School and has hired four new teachers. He decides to implement a new teacher-training program in addition to what the district provides. The program will begin two weeks before the school year starts.

61. What information should Mr. Ross include on the first day of training to *best* acclimate the new teachers?
   a. School profile.
   b. Course teaching assignment, class lists, and room assignment.
   c. Contact information for key people in the event of questions.
   d. Parking space number.

62. During the first month of school, one of the new teachers approaches Mr. Ross and says that she feels totally overwhelmed. Mr. Ross wants to help, but their schedules are such that they cannot find a convenient time to meet. What should Mr. Ross do to help the new teacher?
   a. Meet on Saturday.
   b. Provide the new teacher with a mentor for help in cases such as these.
   c. Stop by the new teacher's classroom during class time.
   d. Ask the teacher to give up her entire planning period to meet.

63. Mr. Ross notices that a veteran teacher is treating a first-year teacher poorly. How can Mr. Ross *best* address and help to change this behavior?
   a. By speaking privately with the veteran teacher.
   b. By micromanaging and being sure that the two teachers do not interact throughout the day.
   c. By forcing the two teachers to sit down together and work through their differences.
   d. By asking the AP to handle the situation.

64. One of the new English teachers is having an issue with a parent about a grade earned on an essay. After several phone calls and emails with the parents, the teacher asks Mr. Ross for help because she does not know what else to say on the subject. What should Mr. Ross do to help the new teacher?
   a. Let the teacher and parents work out the conflict among themselves.
   b. Tell the parents that the teacher was wrong.
   c. Tell the teacher that her grading practices should change.
   d. Support and defend the new teacher in front of the parents.

65. Two teachers are vying for the head basketball coach position at Norrick High School. Both are equally qualified, yet the previous principal chose one teacher for the job because they attended the same college. Now, a new principal has been appointed, and the snubbed teacher wants her to re-open the position. What should the new principal do?
   a. Keep the positions "as is" and help the teacher find another coaching position.
   b. Reverse the previous principal's decision and choose the snubbed teacher.
   c. Eliminate the position entirely and choose someone new.
   d. Do not make any changes at all.

66. Ms. Bean has been principal of a large middle school for the past three years. In her fourth year, she is extremely overwhelmed because there is an accreditation visit occurring in the spring. What is the *first* step Ms. Bean should take to alleviate some of her stress regarding her responsibilities?
   a. Continue to shoulder the burden and raise her stress level; some stress is part of the job.
   b. Delegate to the assistant principals.
   c. Create faculty committees, led by assistant principals, that will be responsible for separate aspects of the accreditation process.
   d. Ask parents and community members to help out.

67. A veteran teacher complains to her principal that she has been assigned a "mentee" in the mentoring program and can't handle the added responsibility. What is the appropriate response for the principal?
   a. Examine the teacher's responsibilities to see if her concerns are valid; if so, address her concerns with collaborative solution planning.
   b. Remove the veteran teacher from the program and do not ask for her assistance on any other initiative in the future.
   c. Ask the mentee if there are any problems between her and the veteran teacher.
   d. Remove the veteran teacher from the program and be sure to tell other faculty members that the teacher is unwilling to help or cooperate.

Questions 68 to 73 pertain to the following chart:

Examine the sample chart below, from a nurse's office in a large middle school with a diverse population:

	December	November	October	Sept.	August
Illness/Health Problems	627	660	844	757	452
Injury Visits (occurred at school)	62	81	108	85	41
Injury Visits (occurred at home)	29	47	57	60	33
Sent Home	33	37	44	51	32
Return to Class	674	729	975	832	482
Medication Doses	174	182	301	275	163
Immunization Checks	0	0	0	0	0
Health Procedures (glucose monitoring, etc.)	382	462	727	581	328
Parent Consultations	261	259	228	230	126
Lice Checks	6	0	1	8	2
Health Management Plans	1	4	32	40	31
Staff Consults re: students	6	9	7	4	5
Employee Sick Visits	22	23	24	25	20
Health Related Screenings	0	579	41	0	0
Referrals (to county nurse)	3	0	1	2	3
SST, IEP, or 504 Meetings	0	0	0	0	0
911 Calls	0	0	0	2	0
Total Visits	728	835	1026	936	555

68. The number of illnesses and health problems went from 452 in the month of August to 844 in the month of October. What conclusion can the principal draw from this data?
   a. Students were getting sick as the seasons changed and flu season began.
   b. Instruction was not meeting the needs of all students, causing them to be bored and visit the nurse's office in order to miss class.
   c. Students did not have appropriate healthcare at home.
   d. Teachers were sending students to the nurse for a variety of reasons.

69. How can the principal *best* address this issue?
    a. Conduct classroom walkthroughs to evaluate instruction.
    b. Email the entire faculty and make them aware of the rise in numbers of students visiting the nurse's office.
    c. Ask the nurse to keep a record of which teachers send the most students.
    d. Create a new policy that places strict requirements visiting the nurse's office.

70. The number of cases of lice rose in September. What is the best way for the principal to communicate this to parents?
    a. Post a message on the school's website.
    b. Call the parents of those students who received lice checks.
    c. Send a letter home to all parents with information on how to stop the spread of lice; post a message on the school's website with the same information.
    d. Have the nurse check each child in the school.

71. What should the principal notice about the number of employee sick visits?
    a. The number has drastically increased.
    b. The number has drastically decreased
    c. The number reflects poor teacher dedication.
    d. The number remains almost the same and is only indicative of true teacher illness or injury.

72. The fact that the nurse was not present at any IEP or 504 meetings for the first half of the school year proves that:
    a. In this particular school, the majority of special education students do not have medical issues.
    b. The school nurse is not required to be at such a meeting.
    c. The nurse is not keeping accurate records.
    d. The nurse should be present, but was not due to an oversight.

73. The number of parent consultations was lowest in August. The fact that the numbers rose is interesting given the fact that the population is very transient. What is one possible explanation for the increase in parental contact?
    a. Parents made themselves more available.
    b. The nurse made more phone calls home.
    c. The school took a more active stance to involve parents.
    d. More students called their parents.

Questions 74 and 75 pertain to the following chart:
The following chart shows the ethnic breakdown of each grade level in a high school.

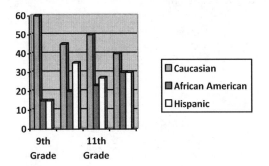

74. The principal has decided there is a need for more intervention programs. Based on this chart, which ethnic groups should be targeted?
   a. Caucasian
   b. Hispanic and Caucasian
   c. Hispanic and African American
   d. Caucasian and African American

75. Based on this same chart, which population showed the biggest growth overall?
   a. Hispanics
   b. Caucasian
   c. African American
   d. Caucasian and Hispanic

76. A sixth grader's parents report repeated bullying of their son on the school bus by three other boys. What is the appropriate response of the principal?
   a. Suspend bus privileges for the three bullies while completing a full investigation.
   b. Have the parents solve the issue on their own time.
   c. Have the students solve the issue during class time.
   d. Have the bus driver solve the issue.

Questions 77 and 78 pertain to the following chart:

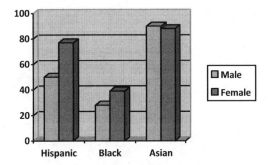

77. Examine the bar graph above. It displays achievement data for minority populations, disaggregated by gender. What population needs the most intervention and help?
    a. asian males
    b. Hispanic females
    c. Black females
    d. Black males

78. What intervention would best serve the at-risk population displayed in this chart?
    a. an after-school mentoring program with academic and social counseling run by teachers with help from community volunteers
    b. Summer school
    c. Extra homework
    d. Remedial classes

79. Due to budget cuts and redistricting, a middle school's student and teacher population will be divided between two other schools. The principal wants to create a new vision of learning for the assimilated students. What groups should he engage to effectively create a new vision and mission?
    a. Parents and teachers
    b. Teachers and students
    c. Community members, teachers, and parents
    d. Community members, teachers, parents, and students

80. There is a gas leak in a high school science classroom. All students, faculty, and staff respond appropriately to the crisis plan and evacuate safely. How should the principal communicate this incident to parents?
    a. Don't mention anything to the parents because no one was injured.
    b. Post a message on the school's website and send a letter home to each parent describing the events and resolution.
    c. Have each teacher call a certain number of parents to relay the news.
    d. Tell the students to tell their parents.

81. It is brought to the attention of a middle school principal that a teacher is not correctly adhering to an Individualized Education Plan. He speaks with the teacher and the issue is resolved. This is an example of:
    a. Strong leadership
    b. Caring personality
    c. Knowledge of legal guidelines pertaining to students with disabilities
    d. Poor leadership

82. Three high school students approach the principal about starting a dance team. They have already secured a faculty adviser. How can the principal effectively coordinate the implementation of this extracurricular activity?
    a. Have the adviser perform all the legwork; check in periodically on progress.
    b. Work collaboratively with the adviser and dance team member to ensure a successful first year; check in periodically on progress.
    c. Allow the students to take on most of the work.
    d. Take on most of the work himself and add more responsibilities to the principal's job.

83. A traditionally small and homogenous elementary school has seen a huge influx of immigrants over the past three years. What is the *first* thing the principal should do to address the new need?
   a. Review current programs.
   b. Survey and ascertain the highest percentage of ethnic groups that have immigrated.
   c. Ask the teachers for ideas on new programs.
   d. Ensure that all current ESOL programs are being implemented according to state and federal guidelines.

84. How can a principal provide the best support and morale to faculty and staff?
   a. Listen objectively to their ideas.
   b. Validate their opinions.
   c. Allow faculty and staff to make important decisions.
   d. Allow staff members to run the faculty meetings.

85. Eighty percent of students fail a standardized department exam throughout the district. At the principals' meeting, the superintendent asks for opinions on what should be done next. What is the *first* step a principal should take?
   a. accuse the teachers of not adequately preparing students.
   b. Examine the test questions and if inappropriate, invalidate the scores.
   c. Accuse the students of not adequately preparing.
   d. Examine the test questions and keep the scores regardless of conclusions drawn.

86. Let's assume the scores are invalidated. What can the principal do to ensure this does not happen again next year?
   a. Meet with teachers and bring their opinions to the county's test writers.
   b. Meet regularly with the test writers to ensure the test is aligned with the standards and curriculum.
   c. Regularly observe students to ensure they are paying attention in class.
   d. Regularly observe teachers to ensure they are providing adequate instruction.

87. It has been determined that the current Social Studies curriculum is not aligned to the majority of state standards. What factors should be *most* considered in adopting a new curriculum?
   a. State standards and requirements
   b. County standards and requirements
   c. Current textbooks
   d. Current program implementation

88. How can a principal ensure that a budget stays in the black?
   a. By securing goods and services before authorizing payment for those goods and services.
   b. By reviewing debt and balance sheets before approving orders to the account.
   c. By requiring vendors to submit competitive bids for goods and services.
   d. By maintaining an organized system for all staff members to record purchases and possession of textbooks, materials, etc.

89. A high school principal has been given an allotment of one new hire for the upcoming school year, yet there is a need for two teachers. What factors will *best* help her determine which departments will receive the new hire?
   a. Teacher requests
   b. Seniority requirements
   c. Student need
   d. Curriculum requirements

90. An administrative assistant is overheard sharing confidential personnel information over the phone. What should the principal do?
   a. Issue a verbal warning.
   b. Issue a written warning.
   c. Act according to the district's confidentiality and personnel clauses; namely, such actions are unacceptable and cause for dismissal.
   d. Give the assistant a second chance.

91. A faculty club adviser is caught stealing funds from the club's account. What is the *first* action the principal should take?
   a. Gather all information before making a decision.
   b. Suspend the teacher pending a full investigation.
   c. Immediately fire the teacher.
   d. Allow the teacher to tell her side of the story.

92. Habitat for Humanity contacts a middle and high school looking for student volunteers. The schools' principals convene and choose the criteria and scheduling for the volunteers. Legally, what do the principals need to do next?
   a. Choose the students who fit their criteria.
   b. Inform the parents of the opportunity.
   c. Ask the teachers for their nominations.
   d. Ask students if they are interested in the opportunity.

93. A custodian fails to post a wet floor sign after mopping the hallway floor, and a teacher slips and breaks her ankle. As principal, what is the appropriate *first* action to take?
   a. Call an attorney.
   b. Call the teacher's family.
   c. Call an ambulance.
   d. Fire the custodian.

94. An elementary school is changing the half-day kindergarten program to a full-day kindergarten. The principal holds a meeting with the kindergarten teachers to discuss the transition. The current teachers want to be on the hiring committee for the new teacher that is to come on board. What is the appropriate response of the principal?
   a. Deny the teachers the opportunity.
   b. Take the teachers' suggestions and use them in the interview process without including the teachers in the actual interview.
   c. Allow them to serve on the interview committee.
   d. Choose teachers from a cross-section of grades to conduct the interview.

95. The kindergarten curriculum must also change. Who should the principal appoint to serve on the committee?
    a. administrators only
    b. Kindergarten teachers only
    c. Kindergarten and first grade teachers
    d. A teacher from each grade level

96. A high school principal wants to implement new initiatives to help student achievement and is examining data to look for areas of weakness. Which of the following is most indicative of ineffective teaching and learning?
    a. Teacher absentee rate
    b. Student report cards
    c. Length of class periods
    d. Percentage of students in ESOL programs

97. Mr. Glen is the new principal of Jones Middle School. The previous principal eliminated the substitute teacher service and required teachers to call for their own subs to eliminate teacher absenteeism. The majority of teachers have approached Mr. Glen to reinstate the sub service. What information should Mr. Glen use to decide whether or not to bring back the service?
    a. Teacher opinion
    b. A comparison of teacher absenteeism before and after the sub service
    c. Student test scores
    d. Referral and discipline rates among different groups of students

98. A teacher is given two days off to attend holiday religious services. The teacher takes a third day off without permission. What is the appropriate response of the principal?
    a. ask the teacher to explain the reason for the infraction.
    b. Refer the teacher to the county office's human resource department.
    c. Let the infraction slide without addressing it.
    d. Give the teacher a consequence as laid out in the personnel clauses of the teacher contract.

99. A massive food fight erupts in a high school cafeteria as part of "Senior Prank." How can the principal restore order and what should the initiating students' punishment be?
    a. Shut all cafeteria doors and not let students enter or exit; students will have to clean up the food; initiating students will be suspended.
    b. Have teachers restrain students; custodians will have to clean up the food.
    c. Let the fight die down; custodians and students will clean up the food.
    d. Shut all cafeteria doors and not let students enter or exit; teachers will have to clean up the food.

Answer Key and Explanations

1. **C:** Consider the objective in this example: to foster positive and collegial relationships among faculty and staff members. A principal should implement strategies to ensure the development of collegial relationships and effective collaboration. As such, option D is not a good strategy to implement because it does not recognize the diverse needs and opinions of staff. Options A and B are valid, but only allow for faculty and staff communication on a periodic basis. Thus, option C is the correct answer because frequent and continuous communication will create and maintain collegial relationships among staff.

2. **B:** If we examine the identified outcome, the effective principal will give parents the chance to be engaged in the educational process of their children. Options A, C, and D do not provide parents with substantial or frequent opportunities to be involved in the educational process. Option B is the correct answer because parents will have frequent interaction with teachers, students, and administrators and will help the campus meet the needs of all students.

3. **C:** A principal should know how to act with integrity, fairness, and in an ethical and legal manner. The main issue in this scenario is one of confidentiality. It is against the confidentiality rights of other students to share their actions and discipline with other parents. Furthermore, a special education meeting is not the venue to discuss such issues with parents. To that end, the correct answer is C. The other choices do not follow any legal or ethical guidelines of school administrators.

4. **B:** The focus of this question is curriculum. A principal should know how to implement curricula that enhances teaching and learning. In order to achieve this goal, a principal must have a solid grasp of current best practices and research. Also, a principal must be aware of current economic and work place trends. While choices A, C, and D are all valid, the *best* answer is B because the principal uses the largest amount of background knowledge, while at the same time surveying the faculty in charge of the curriculum's implementation.

5. **C:** Since the question clearly states that the goal is to effectively meet the needs of all students, choice A is not appropriate because the principal's own agenda would most likely not benefit the students. Also, choice D would not work here because the students' best interests are not the basis of making the decision. While choice B is definitely valid, there are more aspects to consider besides just the number in a grade or the number of teachers available. Therefore, choice C is the correct answer, since a principal should know how to allocate resources effectively and equitably.

6. **C:** The main purpose of a faculty meeting is to improve the performance of all staff members. Choices A and B do not allow for improvement among staff members, and choice D does not promote any positive growth in a school building. Choice C allows staff members to constructively share their concerns while at the same time hold interesting conversations and participate in professional development that, in the long run, will benefit the students.

7. **C:** In adopting a new piece of curriculum, it is important to remember to allocate appropriate time and funding for professional development. In this case, simply handing the teachers the new materials does not allow for appropriate reflection and adoption of new curriculum. Therefore, choice A is not the correct answer. Also, one in-service day consisting of only teachers at Smith Middle School does not ensure great teaching and learning for all students. Choice B is not a bad idea, but is not the *best* answer for this question. Finally, sending all the teachers to a national conference is not the best way to use funds and is not necessary in making a small change such as simply adding ancillary materials to a curriculum. As such, choice C is the correct answer; teachers will be afforded the opportunity to familiarize themselves with the manipulatives, while at the same time learn from colleagues who have already implemented the strategies in the classroom.

8. **D:** Principals should know how to apply organizational, decision-making, and problem-solving skills to ensure an effective learning environment. In the scenario presented above, it is clear that the issue is the absenteeism of the assistant principal, which is directly affecting the safety of the students. As such, choices A and B are not correct because those teachers have already fulfilled their duties and asking them to take on additional responsibilities is not an effective use of organizational knowledge or staff resources. Dismissing fewer students at a time (choice C) is also not correct because that will not solve the problem of the assistant principal. Therefore, choice D is the correct answer because a principal knows how to diagnose personnel issues and appropriately address them to ensure change in behaviors. The collaborative plan will allow the absentee assistant principal the opportunity to change behaviors or accept consequences as put forth by the plan.

9. **C:** In order to manage human and material resources, a principal must be able to keep a level head and not make rash decisions. Principles should apply principles of effective leadership and management; therefore, choices A, B, and D are incorrect because they do not use staff resources appropriately. As with the previous issue of the assistant principal's absenteeism, the issue here is that teachers are stealing from the school. Also, the principal must first be sure that such accusations are correct before taking strict steps to fix an issue that may or may not be present. Knowing how to correctly manage faculty is a crucial skill for any principal. As such, choice C is the correct answer.

10. **B:** A principal should implement strategies that enable the school physical plant to operate safely and effectively. The police do not need to be involved unless the perpetrator is actually caught. So while it would be appropriate to ask the police to monitor the building at night, daily stake outs are not necessary or a proper use of human resources. Neither should the school principal personally stake out the building. Therefore, choices A and C are not correct. Choice D is not appropriate because it puts other students at risk. Choice B is the correct answer because it addresses the concerns and gives students and faculty an active voice in keeping the facility clean.

11. **B:** The correct answer is B because it allows for the development and implementation of crisis procedures. Not only are the procedures clearly written to facilitate easy reference, but practice drills are also held to ensure successful implementation. Choices A and C are good reminders, but not good implementation. Choice D should not be an option, because the intruder should not be made aware of protection plans.

12. **A:** Choice B does not work here because students will naturally gravitate toward their friends; this does not affect their ability to be engaged in the classroom. The number of students in a classroom is certainly a factor, yet is not a solid indication that the students' needs are not being met. Also, students are reluctant to do homework regardless of their needs being met. Therefore, the correct answer is A, because students have not been appropriately placed in classes; this means their needs are not being met and they are acting out because they are either bored or over stimulated.

13. **A:** While choices B, C, and D are all possibilities, they do not address the central issue of inequitable treatment among students. This could lead to some students being referred more often than others, or some not at all, despite the presence of misconduct. Choice A is the correct answer because it will create teacher buy-in and help the students realize the importance of proper behavior. Also, it will eliminate the discrimination previously present in the school's disciplinary policies.

14. **A:** Since Ms. Rose is examining a large discrepancy in the discipline referrals among student groups, the correct answer is A. For those students who choose not to accept their punishment, there is no meaningful consequence, which continues the cycle of poor behavior and discipline referrals. This policy certainly needs revision, as the students need to know that their behavior is unacceptable. Choices B, C, and D are all disciplinary actions that can remain in place to foster a positive school climate.

15. **B:** Since Ms. Rose is concerned with whether or not the students' educational needs are being met, the number enrolled in either extracurricular or sports programs (answers A and C) should not have any bearing on their academic achievement or disciplinary referrals. While extracurricular and sports programs do provide a positive outlet for students, this is not the correct answer for this specific example. The attrition rate (answer D) does not affect this particular scenario, but special education numbers are certainly important when examining data. Ms. Rose needs to ensure that there are proper programs with funding and staffing in place to ensure success for all students. Therefore, the correct answer is B.

16. **B:** As stated in the previous question, Ms. Rose needs to ensure proper staffing and program implementation. Therefore, English as a Second Language enrollment is the most important piece of data for this example. Since we are looking solely at numbers, parental involvement in conferences (answer A) does not always translate to teachers helping meet the needs of all students. Professional development (answer C) is certainly a valuable tool to building teachers' knowledge, but attendance does not tell us much about implementation in the classroom. Also, paraprofessionals (answer D) are a great asset to schools, but their presence does not guarantee that student's needs are being met.

17. **A:** This scenario is concerned with the students who miss class or instructional time. Therefore, pull-out or enrichment classes would have only a slight impact on student achievement, as answer C is concerned with federal education regulations, and answer D deals with enrichment students who are gaining instructional time. Sports programs (answer B) occur after school, so they would not interfere with instructional time. Choice A is the correct answer because students are missing valuable class time ostensibly for non-legitimate reasons. Ms. Rose is now charged with cross-referencing the data to specific teachers and ensuring they are equipped with proper engaging teaching strategies. She must also ensure that students are appropriately placed for their achievement.

18. **B:** B is the correct answer because it is the only one that gives a reason for students missing class time. The other activities usually would not affect the amount of time each student spends in each class.

19. **A:** If students are age-inappropriate for a grade level, placing them in remedial-level classes will not necessarily allow them to be promoted to the next grade. The crux of the issue is what interventions can the school offer to help students succeed in each grade. Choice A of a mandatory mentoring program based on individual weaknesses would certainly help students work through both academic and social issues. So while extra help with teachers could definitely be beneficial, answer A is the one that will *best* address the age-inappropriate issue.

20. **C:** As stated previously, we are looking for the intervention that will *best* address the age-inappropriate issue. Certainly, counseling and coaching will best help students work through issues and become successful students.

21. **C:** Parental support is quite a large part of student success. As such, choice C is the best answer because it allows for the most parental involvement. Also, Ms. Rose would welcome parental involvement as a principal, because parents will help with successful implementation of programs to improve student achievement and disciplinary issues. Choices A, B and D are all valid, but do not offer enough involvement on the part of the parents.

22. **B:** To create teacher buy-in, Ms. Rose should survey the staff and use their ideas to help implement new programs. This will help to foster a positive climate and a unified vision. Therefore, the correct answer is B. Choices A, C, and D are also valid, but will not help Ms. Rose create teacher buy-in.

23. **D:** Choices B and C are not professional. While choice A is definitely a possibility, a stronger way to show areas of growth is to invite critics to the building for a guided tour to demonstrate all the positive changes that have taken place in the building. Therefore, choice D is the best response.

24. **C:** Since the stimulus tells us that Mr. Jones wants to create more elective opportunities and more college-placement courses, the most important piece of data is the percentage of students who attend college. Therefore, the correct answer is C. Certainly, the retention rate once the students are in college is useful, but not for the purposes of this stimulus. The freshman retention rate is also significant, but will not help in determining college placement options for those students who remain in high school. It is assumed that, due to federal education laws, students will not be permitted to drop out of high school as freshmen.

25. **B:** Since the purpose of changing the schedule is to offer more electives, answer B is correct because it will allow Mr. Jones to see what types of electives should be made available to students. For example, should the electives focus on culinary, auto, etc.? This data will be the most useful for these purposes.

26. **B:** A principal should facilitate the development, articulation, implementation, and stewardship of a vision of learning that is shared and supported by the school community. Since the question is asking for the *first* step Mr. Jones should take, options A and C do not

apply because they are strictly top-down approaches to administration, which do not foster a shared vision of learning. Option D is a possibility, but only works in tandem with the ideas presented in option B. Each idea in B will allow Mr. Jones to create a shared vision and will help achieve his long-term goal of improved student achievement and varied course offerings.

27. **C:** A good principal is also an effective manager of human resources. By asking the negative teachers to share their ideas and to have them use their strengths to performs tasks and eventually improve morale, Mr. Jones is applying principles of leadership and management. Therefore, option C is the correct answer. Option A, ignoring the negative teachers, is not supportive and will not achieve the desired result. Option B is certainly feasible, but simply discussing negative responses does not affect change and will also not help to achieve the desired result. Finally, appointing the negative teachers to head the committee is promoting the negative behavior and is giving credence to their negativity.

28. **B:** Obviously, offering monetary incentives is against any moral or ethical standards of a school principal. As such, choice C can be crossed out immediately. While many communities donate money and service to schools, choice D would not help Mr. Jones achieve his objectives. Choice A, surveying community members, can produce useful information but may not help to effect the desired change. Allowing the community members to visit the school and serve on the committee will help make those stakeholders active participants in the educational process. An effective principal will use strategies to involve all stakeholders in planning processes to enable the collaborative development of a shared campus vision focused on teaching and learning. To that end, B is the correct answer.

29. **B:** Creating a cooperative school-to-work program will most likely get community members on board for changing the schedule, as the change would allow students to work in the community and foster positive relationships. Also, such a schedule change will help the local economy while teaching students a valuable skill set. The other options will certainly involve the community, but answer B is the most beneficial and therefore the correct answer.

30. **C:** A principal should facilitate effective campus curriculum planning based on knowledge of various factors, such as emerging issues, etc. Because of this, the correct answer is C. By using research-based methods, Mr. Jones and the faculty will ensure an aligned curriculum that will promote student success.

31. **C:** A principal should know how to implement strategies to ensure the development of collegial relationships and effective collaboration. As such, options A and D will not work because they are completely one-sided and do not develop collegial relationships. While it may work to have the department coordinator weigh in on the issue, asking the coordinator to address the problem is not indicative of effective leadership. Therefore, C is the correct answer because it allows all parties to have an active interest in the decision making process.

32. **B:** It is important for the principal to create a shared vision for student success. Meeting with the involved parties allows for the faculty to create a shared vision for practices such as grading. The other options are one-sided and do not allow for creating a shared vision.

33. **D:** Choices A through C take a passive stance on the issue and will not help to resolve any problems. Personnel management is an essential component of a principal's job. As such, choice D is the answer because it follows legal and moral guidelines to reach a solution.

34. **A:** A principal should know how to implement strategies to provide ongoing support to campus staff. Choices B and C are not acceptable ways of addressing the issue. It is acceptable to issue formal written warnings (choice D), but in this instance doing so will not address the central issue, which is that the principal has no evidence that the teacher has, in fact, said inappropriate things. Therefore, choice A is the correct answer because it ensures support to staff members and adequately addresses the needs of each stakeholder.

35. **C:** A principal should know how to apply principles of leadership and management to the campus physical plant. According to these standards, choice C is the best option here. Choice C will allow the principal to work collaboratively with all stakeholders to resolve the issue.

36. **D:** Answer D applies best to the "Character Counts" program in which students are taught tolerance and proper behaviors for a global society and economy.

37. **C:** Since the question involves student interest and enrollment, C is the correct answer because it addresses all aspects of program adoption. A school must first determine whether a program is feasible both financially and in terms of human resources before it can be adopted.

38. **B:** In this instance, neither positive nor negative reinforcement is apt to raise enrollment numbers. The real way to increase enrollment is to educate all stakeholders and demonstrate the benefits available to those students who enroll in such a course. Therefore, B is the correct answer.

39. **C:** Since the program is, no doubt, being adopted with the students' best interest in mind, it would not be wise for the principal to send only those teachers who are his friends. Furthermore, only sending department coordinators or those with seniority will not be most beneficial to the students or staff. By sending a cross-section, the principal is ensuring that all grades and content areas are being represented. Each teacher can then return to school and share what he or she has learned at the conference. The principal can then rotate through cross-sections until all teachers have received the training.

40. **B:** A vision must include buy-in from all stakeholder groups: staff, parents, students, and community members. By providing a forum in which frank and open discussion can occur, the principal will allow for effective creation of a new mission and vision that everyone will support. Just asking one group will not create a feeling of community or a shared vision. Therefore, the answer is B.

41. **B:** Teachers can definitely learn best from each other and by observing good teaching practices. Simply reading articles or attending workshops or professional development programs will not allow teachers to acquire the appropriate skill set. Answer B, teacher observation, is the correct answer.

42. **B:** Scope and sequence among all grade levels and content areas is the most important asset to any curriculum program. It is completely unfair to say that the programs are too hard or too easy, or that the students lose interest in school as they get older. Therefore, the correct answer is B.

43. **C:** Student achievement can *almost* always be directly correlated to effective teaching strategies. It is certainly possible that the elementary teachers have prepared the students well for middle school. Thus, the most plausible answer is choice C, because the middle school teachers are clearly meeting the needs of all students.

44. **A:** Since this scenario involves supporting teachers, a training video (answer B) would not be good support. Also, continuing to use the same methods (answer C) would definitely not be appropriate because the student population is changing. Professional development (answer D) may be somewhat effective, but the only way to really ensure quality teaching practices is to show teachers good examples of what they are expected to do. Therefore, the correct answer is A.

45. **D:** A principal should know how to apply principles of effective leadership and management in relation to campus personnel and resource utilization. Therefore, the answer is D.

46. **A:** The scenario is asking about open communication. Thus, the answer is A because a respectful atmosphere can best lead to open communication. The other options may be applicable, but the *best* answer is A.

47. **C:** The only way to promote ownership is to use ideas that come from each group, which means that the correct answer is C. Even if ideas proposed at the curriculum meetings are not used, the gatherings are a way to validate everyone's opinions. The other options are too close-minded and will not promote ownership.

48. **B:** The biggest concern in any school is student safety. As such, the decisions regarding space should be made with the students' best interest in mind, regardless of staff preferences. Answer B is the only one that will allow this to happen.

49. **B:** While answers A, C, and D can certainly apply to most situations, we are concerned here with the principal's main priority. In order to best serve his staff and create a collaborative community, he needs to understand and appreciate their talents.

50. **A:** Negativity is a common opponent in the principal's job. Going behind the AP's back to ask questions about him will only further damage the relationship. In order to build a good working relationship, the principal must validate the assistant principal's skills and allow him to flourish. Delegating will not accomplish this task. Therefore, the answer is A.

51. **B:** We are concerned here with creating representation for both schools. Therefore, the correct answer is B because it will allow both current PTAs to have a say in forming the new PTA. The other options are one-sided and will not allow for equal representation.

52. **B:** By using negative methods, the principal will only create more negative feelings. But by inviting the community member to tour the school, he can use a positive action to reverse negative feelings and to forge a cooperative relationship with the community.

53. **C:** It is possible that the teachers are non-compliant for a whole host of reasons. Before sending terse or direct emails, it is best to address non-compliance personally. Also, delegating such a responsibility to an AP does not exemplify good leadership. The correct answer is C because it allows the principal to properly address the issue.

54. **D:** It is not appropriate to punish the whole staff for something that only a few teachers are doing. By emailing the entire staff (answer C), the principal is not sending a message conducive to community. Also, placing written warnings (answer A) or highlighted contractual passages (answer B) in mailboxes is a very passive way to be a leader. A true and effective leader will be active and address issues head on. Thus, the answer is D.

55. **C:** C is the correct answer because it uses stakeholder feedback while compensating the adviser with a small stipend to say that her time is valuable.
Allowing students to create policies and practices (answer D) is not a valid practice for a principal. Answer A, while using stakeholder feedback, does not recognize the adviser's time. Offering money to the adviser (answer B) will not allow for student-centered activities.

56. **B:** Firing the teacher (answer C) and informing the police (answer A) may be options, but first the principal has to comply with the formal policies of the district. As such, the answer is B. Informing the media (answer D) is completely inappropriate.

57. **B:** The very first thing the principal should do is to ascertain the condition of the child, since children's safety is a principal's number-one priority. The other actions may follow, depending on district policy, but the question here is asking what the principal should do first. Thus, the answer is B.

58. **A:** Without first examining the district's suspension policy, choice D is not appropriate. It also not appropriate to take either side without ascertaining what exactly happened. Therefore, choice A is the correct answer.

59. **B:** B is the correct answer, because using quantitative and qualitative data based on the observation will give the teacher a foundation on which to change his teaching practices. Making demands (answer A) and writing complaints (answer C) will not forge a solid working relationship. Involving other teachers (answer D) is not appropriate, nor will it solve the issue.

60. **C:** A principal should know how to effectively hire staff. In this situation, the teacher's educational philosophy (answer C) is the most important, because the teacher will be joining a new school and assimilating with that school's current mission and vision. In order to meet the needs of all students, a teacher must have a corresponding educational philosophy. The other answers are certainly considerations, but the question is looking at the most important aspect, which surely is educational philosophy.

61. **B:** B is the correct order because in order to best acclimate the new teachers on the first day, they need the basic information required to help set up their new classrooms and begin planning units and lessons. It is assumed they already are aware of the school profile and will receive other such information during the district's training. The contact list will come in handy, but it is not the very first thing a new teacher requires.

62. **B:** The best solution is to provide the new teacher with a mentor who is able to guide and help the new teacher. Asking the new teacher to give up an entire planning period will most likely overwhelm her. Meeting on Saturdays is not usually feasible, nor is asking the teacher to give up valuable class time.

63. **A:** While it is acceptable and even encouraged to delegate to the AP (answer D), doing so in this scenario would not solve the issue. Neither forcing distance between the two teachers (answer C) nor forcing them to sit face- to-face (answer B) will solve the issue, as one is classic avoidance and the other is classic confrontation. Thus, the best idea is to speak privately with the veteran teacher (answer A) in an attempt to alleviate the situation.

64. **D:** It is crucial to always support staff and create a unified front when dealing with outside stakeholders. The correct answer is to support the teacher and her grading practices. Of course, if there is a larger issue, that can be dealt with without the parents being present.

65. **A:** The correct answer is A because the principal should keep the staffing positions "as is," at least long enough to gather substantive information about the position. Choice A also lets the principal help the teacher break into coaching, which is important to the teacher. It is bad practice to completely reverse decisions made by previous principals (answer B). In some cases, a reversal may be warranted, but in this case, there have been no complaints about the current coach. Not choosing either teacher is not an option (answer C); neither is not making any changes at all (answer D).

66. **C:** We are concerned here with Ms. Bean alleviating her stress. Completely ignoring the situation or delegating completely will not help the situation, and would, in fact, create more stress. Creating faculty committees led by assistant principals will allow the principal to maintain an active role in the process while allowing teachers and APs to do the same.

67. **A:** A principal should model and promote the highest standard of conduct, ethical principles, and integrity in decision making, actions, and behaviors. In keeping with this definition, answer A is appropriate because it addresses the issue in a mature and proper way without involving outside parties. Never asking for her help again (answer B) will not solve any issues, nor will involving the mentee (answer C), who is clearly busy with first-year teaching duties. Sharing information with faculty members (answer D) is extremely unprofessional.

68. **B:** While the other options are certainly possibilities, the most likely cause of the rise in visits to the nurse is boredom in or avoidance of the classroom (answer B). As instruction and content material becomes harder in the second quarter of school, student behavior will change.

69. **A:** A is the correct answer because visiting classrooms to be aware of what is happening in the building is the best way to address the issue. Emailing the entire faculty (answer B) and creating new policies (answer D) will not foster an atmosphere of respect in the decision-making process. Asking the school nurse to keep track of which teachers send the most students (answer C) is not an effective use of time.

70. **C:** A principal should be able to communicate effectively with all stakeholder groups. The best answer is C because it is a two-pronged approach to getting the message to

parents. It is not a good use of human resources to have the nurse check every single student, nor is it appropriate to only post a message or to only contact those parents whose children are already being treated. It is also important to remember confidentiality laws in this situation.

71. **D:** At times, data serves to show us that a school is running smoothly. An average of 23 teacher visits to the nurse's office seems about average for a school of this size. Also, the fact that the numbers do not really fluctuate demonstrate that teachers are not responding emotionally or passively to events in the district or school, but that they are, in fact, in need of medical attention.

72. **D:** The most likely answer in this scenario is D. It is quite unusual that every single special education student would not have a medical issue. Also, the nurse is required to be at meetings if the student has a health issue, and the records appear to be accurate in all other columns. Therefore, the principal is not aware of the requirements of such a meeting.

73. **C:** The other answers are possible, but the most plausible explanation is that the school took a more active stance to involve parents in the occurrences at school.

74. **C:** While we do not want to overlook the Caucasian population, the question specifically cites intervention programs, which most usually means for those segments of the school population that have the least amount of representation. Since Caucasians have the most representation, we can eliminate any answer with Caucasian as a choice, and therefore choice C is the correct answer.

75. **A:** The Hispanic population showed the biggest growth overall, while the Caucasian population showed the greatest decline. Thus, the answer is A.

76. **A:** A is the appropriate response because it follows all legal and ethical guidelines to solve an issue brought to light by concerned parents.

77. **D:** According to the chart, the population with the lowest achievement rate is black males.

78. **A:** A is the correct answer because the only way to effectively address this issue is to help the students with every aspect of their lives and to involve as many stakeholders as possible. The other options will not help the students, because they do not address the root causes for the problem.

79. **D:** An effective principal will engage all four stakeholder groups in order to create and implement a mission and vision. All options except D eliminate one of the key stakeholders.

80. **B:** A principal should know how to communicate effectively with families and other community members in varied educational contexts. Answers A and D are not examples of effective communication and answer C is a misuse of time and resources.

81. **C:** While the principal's behavior is an example of strong leadership and a caring personality, those are not the *best* answer for this question. The correct answer is C.

82. **B:** The effective principal knows how to manage human resources. The best way to achieve solid management in this scenario is to work with all groups and periodically review progress. Allowing only one group to take on all the work is poor time and resource management, as well as ineffective leadership.

83. **D:** The question asks what the principal must do *first*. Because of this, the correct answer is to ensure that all programs are meeting state and federal guidelines. Federal mandates are quite important, and a principal must have a solid grasp of all rules and regulations before implementing new programs. It is important to have the data listed in choices A and B, but the first thing to do is to make sure a school has the resources to properly implement a program.

84. **B:** A principal should know how to acknowledge and celebrate the contributions of staff. In keeping with this definition, the principal must first validate staff members and make them believe themselves to be valuable members of the community.

85. **B:** Sometimes the error is on the part of the test, not the students or teachers. Keep in mind that in this scenario, eighty percent of students failed, which is an extreme majority in terms of test taking. It would be unfair to blame teachers for not instructing or students for not preparing. Also, if the test is determined to be unfair, it would not be wise to keep the scores regardless. Therefore, invalidating the scores would be the best option here.

86. **B:** Since the scores were invalidated, obviously the problem lies with the test itself. By meeting with test writers, the principal can ensure that test questions adequately cover the existing standards and curriculum Neither the teachers nor the students are at fault in this instance and therefore it would not behoove the principal to look for problems where none exist.

87. **A:** State standards should be first considered when aligning curriculums with state tests. Then, the question should be "how can we best ensure student achievement under these guidelines?" Current textbooks and programs certainly pull some weight, but curriculums must change with the times. County and local standards are also important, but the *most* important factor is the state requirements.

88. **B:** A principal should know how to apply principles of effective leadership and management in relation to campus budgeting. While certainly all options can help maintain solid banking practices, option B will best allow the principal to do so because under this system, he will always know how much money is in an account.

89. **C:** Students' needs should always be the driving force behind decisions made on school campuses. Safety is the number one concern, followed by providing services and programs that meet the needs of all learners.

90. **C:** A principal should be well-versed in confidentiality guidelines and will act accordingly. As such, the answer is C because a principal must always check with legal guidelines before making formal and irreversible decisions.

91. **B:** An action such as stealing requires suspension pending a full investigation. It would not be appropriate to immediately fire the teacher, nor to allow her to tell her side of the story without the presence of a lawyer.

92. **B:** Legally, parents must be informed before any formal decisions can be made. Therefore, the correct answer is B.

93. **C:** The safety and well-being of students and staff are the very first priorities of any school building. Therefore, the first thing a principal should do is call an ambulance to help the injured teacher.

94. **C:** The kindergarten teachers should be afforded the opportunity to interview the new teacher, because they will be working closely together. Denying them the opportunity will not help create a unified vision, and using their suggestions without their presence is bad leadership practice. Therefore, the correct answer is C.

95. **C:** The committee should be comprised of kindergarten and first grade teachers, because they are most responsible for implementation and cohesion. Including representatives from all grade levels is not necessary because the kindergarten and first grade teachers can use their curriculums to guide their practice in order to create dovetailing curriculums. Thus, C is the correct answer.

96. **A:** The teacher absentee rate is the most important piece of data because it is a symptom of a larger problem. If the absentee rate is high, then teachers are passively avoiding work, ostensibly for a variety of reasons. The grades, ESOL programs, and amount of instructional time do not have as much to do with weaknesses as the absentee rate.

97. **B:** The previous principal was attempting to reduce the amount of teacher absenteeism. The only way to decide whether or not to reinstate the service is to compare the data before and after the service was in place. Therefore, B is the correct answer.

98. **D:** It is certainly not appropriate for the principal to not address the issue; this is passive and will not create a respectful environment among colleagues. The teacher's explanation may give some insight into the action, but will not excuse the behavior. The correct response is D, because a principal must always be aware of contractual obligations and legal guidelines.

99. **A:** The only acceptable response in this situation is for the students to take full responsibility for their actions and to accept the consequence of suspension for fighting in school. Asking the custodians or teachers to clean up will not solve any issue, nor will having teachers restrain students or letting the fight run its course. Thus, the correct answer is A.

Secret Key #1 - Time is Your Greatest Enemy

Pace Yourself

Wear a watch. At the beginning of the test, check the time (or start a chronometer on your watch to count the minutes), and check the time after every few questions to make sure you are "on schedule."

If you are forced to speed up, do it efficiently. Usually one or more answer choices can be eliminated without too much difficulty. Above all, don't panic. Don't speed up and just begin guessing at random choices. By pacing yourself, and continually monitoring your progress against your watch, you will always know exactly how far ahead or behind you are with your available time. If you find that you are one minute behind on the test, don't skip one question without spending any time on it, just to catch back up. Take 15 fewer seconds on the next four questions, and after four questions you'll have caught back up. Once you catch back up, you can continue working each problem at your normal pace.

Furthermore, don't dwell on the problems that you were rushed on. If a problem was taking up too much time and you made a hurried guess, it must be difficult. The difficult questions are the ones you are most likely to miss anyway, so it isn't a big loss. It is better to end with more time than you need than to run out of time.

Lastly, sometimes it is beneficial to slow down if you are constantly getting ahead of time. You are always more likely to catch a careless mistake by working more slowly than quickly, and among very high-scoring test takers (those who are likely to have lots of time left over), careless errors affect the score more than mastery of material.

Secret Key #2 - Guessing is not Guesswork

You probably know that guessing is a good idea - unlike other standardized tests, there is no penalty for getting a wrong answer. Even if you have no idea about a question, you still have a 20-25% chance of getting it right.

Most test takers do not understand the impact that proper guessing can have on their score. Unless you score extremely high, guessing will significantly contribute to your final score.

Monkeys Take the Test

What most test takers don't realize is that to insure that 20-25% chance, you have to guess randomly. If you put 20 monkeys in a room to take this test, assuming they answered once per question and behaved themselves, on average they would get 20-25% of the questions correct. Put 20 test takers in the room, and the average will be much lower among guessed questions. Why?

1. The test writers intentionally writes deceptive answer choices that "look" right. A test taker has no idea about a question, so picks the "best looking" answer, which is often wrong. The monkey has no idea what looks good and what doesn't, so will

consistently be lucky about 20-25% of the time.
2. Test takers will eliminate answer choices from the guessing pool based on a hunch or intuition. Simple but correct answers often get excluded, leaving a 0% chance of being correct. The monkey has no clue, and often gets lucky with the best choice.

This is why the process of elimination endorsed by most test courses is flawed and detrimental to your performance- test takers don't guess, they make an ignorant stab in the dark that is usually worse than random.

$5 Challenge

Let me introduce one of the most valuable ideas of this course- the $5 challenge:

You only mark your "best guess" if you are willing to bet $5 on it.
You only eliminate choices from guessing if you are willing to bet $5 on it.

Why $5? Five dollars is an amount of money that is small yet not insignificant, and can really add up fast (20 questions could cost you $100). Likewise, each answer choice on one question of the test will have a small impact on your overall score, but it can really add up to a lot of points in the end.

The process of elimination IS valuable. The following shows your chance of guessing it right:

If you eliminate wrong answer choices until only this many answer choices remain:	Chance of getting it correct:
1	100%
2	50%
3	33%

However, if you accidentally eliminate the right answer or go on a hunch for an incorrect answer, your chances drop dramatically: to 0%. By guessing among all the answer choices, you are GUARANTEED to have a shot at the right answer.

That's why the $5 test is so valuable- if you give up the advantage and safety of a pure guess, it had better be worth the risk.

What we still haven't covered is how to be sure that whatever guess you make is truly random. Here's the easiest way:

Always pick the first answer choice among those remaining.

Such a technique means that you have decided, **before you see a single test question**, exactly how you are going to guess- and since the order of choices tells you nothing about which one is correct, this guessing technique is perfectly random.

This section is not meant to scare you away from making educated guesses or eliminating choices- you just need to define when a choice is worth eliminating. The $5 test, along with a pre-defined random guessing strategy, is the best way to make sure you reap all of the benefits of guessing.

Secret Key #3 - Practice Smarter, Not Harder

Many test takers delay the test preparation process because they dread the awful amounts of practice time they think necessary to succeed on the test. We have refined an effective method that will take you only a fraction of the time.

There are a number of "obstacles" in your way to succeed. Among these are answering questions, finishing in time, and mastering test-taking strategies. All must be executed on the day of the test at peak performance, or your score will suffer. The test is a mental marathon that has a large impact on your future.

Just like a marathon runner, it is important to work your way up to the full challenge. So first you just worry about questions, and then time, and finally strategy:

Success Strategy

1. Find a good source for practice tests.
2. If you are willing to make a larger time investment, consider using more than one study guide- often the different approaches of multiple authors will help you "get" difficult concepts.
3. Take a practice test with no time constraints, with all study helps "open book." Take your time with questions and focus on applying strategies.
4. Take a practice test with time constraints, with all guides "open book."
5. Take a final practice test with no open material and time limits

If you have time to take more practice tests, just repeat step 5. By gradually exposing yourself to the full rigors of the test environment, you will condition your mind to the stress of test day and maximize your success.

Secret Key #4 - **Prepare, Don't Procrastinate**

Let me state an obvious fact: if you take the test three times, you will get three different scores. This is due to the way you feel on test day, the level of preparedness you have, and, despite the test writers' claims to the contrary, some tests WILL be easier for you than others.

Since your future depends so much on your score, you should maximize your chances of success. In order to maximize the likelihood of success, you've got to prepare in advance. This means taking practice tests and spending time learning the information and test taking strategies you will need to succeed.

Never take the test as a "practice" test, expecting that you can just take it again if you need to. Feel free to take sample tests on your own, but when you go to take the official test, be prepared, be focused, and do your best the first time!

Secret Key #5 - Test Yourself

Everyone knows that time is money. There is no need to spend too much of your time or too little of your time preparing for the test. You should only spend as much of your precious time preparing as is necessary for you to get the score you need.

Once you have taken a practice test under real conditions of time constraints, then you will know if you are ready for the test or not.

If you have scored extremely high the first time that you take the practice test, then there is not much point in spending countless hours studying. You are already there.

Benchmark your abilities by retaking practice tests and seeing how much you have improved. Once you score high enough to guarantee success, then you are ready.

If you have scored well below where you need, then knuckle down and begin studying in earnest. Check your improvement regularly through the use of practice tests under real conditions. Above all, don't worry, panic, or give up. The key is perseverance!
Then, when you go to take the test, remain confident and remember how well you did on the practice tests. If you can score high enough on a practice test, then you can do the same on the real thing.

General Strategies

The most important thing you can do is to ignore your fears and jump into the test immediately- do not be overwhelmed by any strange-sounding terms. You have to jump into the test like jumping into a pool- all at once is the easiest way.

Make Predictions

As you read and understand the question, try to guess what the answer will be. Remember that several of the answer choices are wrong, and once you begin reading them, your mind will immediately become cluttered with answer choices designed to throw you off. Your mind is typically the most focused immediately after you have read the question and digested its contents. If you can, try to predict what the correct answer will be. You may be surprised at what you can predict.

Quickly scan the choices and see if your prediction is in the listed answer choices. If it is, then you can be quite confident that you have the right answer. It still won't hurt to check the other answer choices, but most of the time, you've got it!

Answer the Question

It may seem obvious to only pick answer choices that answer the question, but the test writers can create some excellent answer choices that are wrong. Don't pick an answer just because it sounds right, or you believe it to be true. It MUST answer the question. Once you've made your selection, always go back and check it against the question and make sure that you didn't misread the question, and the answer choice does answer the question posed.

Benchmark

After you read the first answer choice, decide if you think it sounds correct or not. If it doesn't, move on to the next answer choice. If it does, mentally mark that answer choice. This doesn't mean that you've definitely selected it as your answer choice, it just means that it's the best you've seen thus far. Go ahead and read the next choice. If the next choice is worse than the one you've already selected, keep going to the next answer choice. If the next choice is better than the choice you've already selected, mentally mark the new answer choice as your best guess.

The first answer choice that you select becomes your standard. Every other answer choice must be benchmarked against that standard. That choice is correct until proven otherwise by another answer choice beating it out. Once you've decided that no other answer choice seems as good, do one final check to ensure that your answer choice answers the question posed.

Valid Information

Don't discount any of the information provided in the question. Every piece of information may be necessary to determine the correct answer. None of the information in the question is there to throw you off (while the answer choices will certainly have information to throw you off). If two seemingly unrelated topics are discussed, don't ignore either. You can be confident there is a relationship, or it wouldn't be included in the question, and you are

- 95 -

probably going to have to determine what is that relationship to find the answer.

Avoid "Fact Traps"

Don't get distracted by a choice that is factually true. Your search is for the answer that answers the question. Stay focused and don't fall for an answer that is true but incorrect. Always go back to the question and make sure you're choosing an answer that actually answers the question and is not just a true statement. An answer can be factually correct, but it MUST answer the question asked. Additionally, two answers can both be seemingly correct, so be sure to read all of the answer choices, and make sure that you get the one that BEST answers the question.

Milk the Question

Some of the questions may throw you completely off. They might deal with a subject you have not been exposed to, or one that you haven't reviewed in years. While your lack of knowledge about the subject will be a hindrance, the question itself can give you many clues that will help you find the correct answer. Read the question carefully and look for clues. Watch particularly for adjectives and nouns describing difficult terms or words that you don't recognize. Regardless of if you completely understand a word or not, replacing it with a synonym either provided or one you more familiar with may help you to understand what the questions are asking. Rather than wracking your mind about specific detailed information concerning a difficult term or word, try to use mental substitutes that are easier to understand.

The Trap of Familiarity

Don't just choose a word because you recognize it. On difficult questions, you may not recognize a number of words in the answer choices. The test writers don't put "make-believe" words on the test; so don't think that just because you only recognize all the words in one answer choice means that answer choice must be correct. If you only recognize words in one answer choice, then focus on that one. Is it correct? Try your best to determine if it is correct. If it is, that is great, but if it doesn't, eliminate it. Each word and answer choice you eliminate increases your chances of getting the question correct, even if you then have to guess among the unfamiliar choices.

Eliminate Answers

Eliminate choices as soon as you realize they are wrong. But be careful! Make sure you consider all of the possible answer choices. Just because one appears right, doesn't mean that the next one won't be even better! The test writers will usually put more than one good answer choice for every question, so read all of them. Don't worry if you are stuck between two that seem right. By getting down to just two remaining possible choices, your odds are now 50/50. Rather than wasting too much time, play the odds. You are guessing, but guessing wisely, because you've been able to knock out some of the answer choices that you know are wrong. If you are eliminating choices and realize that the last answer choice you are left with is also obviously wrong, don't panic. Start over and consider each choice again. There may easily be something that you missed the first time and will realize on the second pass.

Tough Questions

If you are stumped on a problem or it appears too hard or too difficult, don't waste time.

Move on! Remember though, if you can quickly check for obviously incorrect answer choices, your chances of guessing correctly are greatly improved. Before you completely give up, at least try to knock out a couple of possible answers. Eliminate what you can and then guess at the remaining answer choices before moving on.

Brainstorm

If you get stuck on a difficult question, spend a few seconds quickly brainstorming. Run through the complete list of possible answer choices. Look at each choice and ask yourself, "Could this answer the question satisfactorily?" Go through each answer choice and consider it independently of the other. By systematically going through all possibilities, you may find something that you would otherwise overlook. Remember that when you get stuck, it's important to try to keep moving.

Read Carefully

Understand the problem. Read the question and answer choices carefully. Don't miss the question because you misread the terms. You have plenty of time to read each question thoroughly and make sure you understand what is being asked. Yet a happy medium must be attained, so don't waste too much time. You must read carefully, but efficiently.

Face Value

When in doubt, use common sense. Always accept the situation in the problem at face value. Don't read too much into it. These problems will not require you to make huge leaps of logic. The test writers aren't trying to throw you off with a cheap trick. If you have to go beyond creativity and make a leap of logic in order to have an answer choice answer the question, then you should look at the other answer choices. Don't overcomplicate the problem by creating theoretical relationships or explanations that will warp time or space. These are normal problems rooted in reality. It's just that the applicable relationship or explanation may not be readily apparent and you have to figure things out. Use your common sense to interpret anything that isn't clear.

Prefixes

If you're having trouble with a word in the question or answer choices, try dissecting it. Take advantage of every clue that the word might include. Prefixes and suffixes can be a huge help. Usually they allow you to determine a basic meaning. Pre- means before, post- means after, pro - is positive, de- is negative. From these prefixes and suffixes, you can get an idea of the general meaning of the word and try to put it into context. Beware though of any traps. Just because con is the opposite of pro, doesn't necessarily mean congress is the opposite of progress!

Hedge Phrases

Watch out for critical "hedge" phrases, such as likely, may, can, will often, sometimes, often, almost, mostly, usually, generally, rarely, sometimes. Question writers insert these hedge phrases to cover every possibility. Often an answer choice will be wrong simply because it leaves no room for exception. Avoid answer choices that have definitive words like "exactly," and "always".

Switchback Words

Stay alert for "switchbacks". These are the words and phrases frequently used to alert you to shifts in thought. The most common switchback word is "but". Others include although, however, nevertheless, on the other hand, even though, while, in spite of, despite, regardless of.

New Information

Correct answer choices will rarely have completely new information included. Answer choices typically are straightforward reflections of the material asked about and will directly relate to the question. If a new piece of information is included in an answer choice that doesn't even seem to relate to the topic being asked about, then that answer choice is likely incorrect. All of the information needed to answer the question is usually provided for you, and so you should not have to make guesses that are unsupported or choose answer choices that require unknown information that cannot be reasoned on its own.

Time Management

On technical questions, don't get lost on the technical terms. Don't spend too much time on any one question. If you don't know what a term means, then since you don't have a dictionary, odds are you aren't going to get much further. You should immediately recognize terms as whether or not you know them. If you don't, work with the other clues that you have, the other answer choices and terms provided, but don't waste too much time trying to figure out a difficult term.

Contextual Clues

Look for contextual clues. An answer can be right but not correct. The contextual clues will help you find the answer that is most right and is correct. Understand the context in which a phrase or statement is made. This will help you make important distinctions.

Don't Panic

Panicking will not answer any questions for you. Therefore, it isn't helpful. When you first see the question, if your mind goes blank, take a deep breath. Force yourself to mechanically go through the steps of solving the problem and using the strategies you've learned.

Pace Yourself

Don't get clock fever. It's easy to be overwhelmed when you're looking at a page full of questions, your mind is full of random thoughts and feeling confused, and the clock is ticking down faster than you would like. Calm down and maintain the pace that you have set for yourself. As long as you are on track by monitoring your pace, you are guaranteed to have enough time for yourself. When you get to the last few minutes of the test, it may seem like you won't have enough time left, but if you only have as many questions as you should have left at that point, then you're right on track!

Answer Selection

The best way to pick an answer choice is to eliminate all of those that are wrong, until only one is left and confirm that is the correct answer. Sometimes though, an answer choice may immediately look right. Be careful! Take a second to make sure that the other choices are not equally obvious. Don't make a hasty mistake. There are only two times that you should stop before checking other answers. First is when you are positive that the answer choice you have selected is correct. Second is when time is almost out and you have to make a quick guess!

Check Your Work

Since you will probably not know every term listed and the answer to every question, it is important that you get credit for the ones that you do know. Don't miss any questions through careless mistakes. If at all possible, try to take a second to look back over your answer selection and make sure you've selected the correct answer choice and haven't made a costly careless mistake (such as marking an answer choice that you didn't mean to mark). This quick double check should more than pay for itself in caught mistakes for the time it costs.

Beware of Directly Quoted Answers

Sometimes an answer choice will repeat word for word a portion of the question or reference section. However, beware of such exact duplication – it may be a trap! More than likely, the correct choice will paraphrase or summarize a point, rather than being exactly the same wording.

Slang

Scientific sounding answers are better than slang ones. An answer choice that begins "To compare the outcomes…" is much more likely to be correct than one that begins "Because some people insisted…"

Extreme Statements

Avoid wild answers that throw out highly controversial ideas that are proclaimed as established fact. An answer choice that states the "process should be used in certain situations, if…" is much more likely to be correct than one that states the "process should be discontinued completely." The first is a calm rational statement and doesn't even make a definitive, uncompromising stance, using a hedge word "if" to provide wiggle room, whereas the second choice is a radical idea and far more extreme.

Answer Choice Families

When you have two or more answer choices that are direct opposites or parallels, one of them is usually the correct answer. For instance, if one answer choice states "x increases" and another answer choice states "x decreases" or "y increases," then those two or three answer choices are very similar in construction and fall into the same family of answer choices. A family of answer choices is when two or three answer choices are very similar in construction, and yet often have a directly opposite meaning. Usually the correct answer choice will be in that family of answer choices. The "odd man out" or answer choice that doesn't seem to fit the parallel construction of the other answer choices is more likely to be incorrect.

Special Report: What Your Test Score Will Tell You About Your IQ

Did you know that most standardized tests correlate very strongly with IQ? In fact, your general intelligence is a better predictor of your success than any other factor, and most tests intentionally measure this trait to some degree to ensure that those selected by the test are truly qualified for the test's purposes.

Before we can delve into the relation between your test score and IQ, I will first have to explain what exactly is IQ. Here's the formula:

Your IQ = 100 + (Number of standard deviations below or above the average)*15

Now, let's define standard deviations by using an example. If we have 5 people with 5 different heights, then first we calculate the average. Let's say the average was 65 inches. The standard deviation is the "average distance" away from the average of each of the members. It is a direct measure of variability - if the 5 people included Jackie Chan and Shaquille O'Neal, obviously there's a lot more variability in that group than a group of 5 sisters who are all within 6 inches in height of each other. The standard deviation uses a number to characterize the average range of difference within a group.

A convenient feature of most groups is that they have a "normal" distribution- makes sense that most things would be normal, right? Without getting into a bunch of statistical mumbo-jumbo, you just need to know that if you know the average of the group and the standard deviation, you can successfully predict someone's percentile rank in the group.

Confused? Let me give you an example. If instead of 5 people's heights, we had 100 people, we could figure out their rank in height JUST by knowing the average, standard deviation, and their height. We wouldn't need to know each person's height and manually rank them, we could just predict their rank based on three numbers.

What this means is that you can take your PERCENTILE rank that is often given with your test and relate this to your RELATIVE IQ of people taking the test - that is, your IQ relative to the people taking the test. Obviously, there's no way to know your actual IQ because the people taking a standardized test are usually not very good samples of the general population- many of those with extremely low IQ's never achieve a level of success or competency necessary to complete a typical standardized test. In fact, professional psychologists who measure IQ actually have to use non-written tests that can fairly measure the IQ of those not able to complete a traditional test.

The bottom line is to not take your test score too seriously, but it is fun to compute your "relative IQ" among the people who took the test with you. I've done the calculations below. Just look up your percentile rank in the left and then you'll see your "relative IQ" for your test in the right hand column-

Percentile Rank	Your Relative IQ		Percentile Rank	Your Relative IQ
99	135		59	103
98	131		58	103
97	128		57	103
96	126		56	102
95	125		55	102
94	123		54	102
93	122		53	101
92	121		52	101
91	120		51	100
90	119		50	100
89	118		49	100
88	118		48	99
87	117		47	99
86	116		46	98
85	116		45	98
84	115		44	98
83	114		43	97
82	114		42	97
81	113		41	97
80	113		40	96
79	112		39	96
78	112		38	95
77	111		37	95
76	111		36	95
75	110		35	94
74	110		34	94
73	109		33	93
72	109		32	93
71	108		31	93
70	108		30	92
69	107		29	92
68	107		28	91
67	107		27	91
66	106		26	90
65	106		25	90
64	105		24	89
63	105		23	89
62	105		22	88
61	104		21	88
60	104		20	87

Special Report: How to Overcome Test Anxiety

The very nature of tests caters to some level of anxiety, nervousness or tension, just as we feel for any important event that occurs in our lives. A little bit of anxiety or nervousness can be a good thing. It helps us with motivation, and makes achievement just that much sweeter. However, too much anxiety can be a problem; especially if it hinders our ability to function and perform.

"Test anxiety," is the term that refers to the emotional reactions that some test-takers experience when faced with a test or exam. Having a fear of testing and exams is based upon a rational fear, since the test-taker's performance can shape the course of an academic career. Nevertheless, experiencing excessive fear of examinations will only interfere with the test-takers ability to perform, and his/her chances to be successful.

There are a large variety of causes that can contribute to the development and sensation of test anxiety. These include, but are not limited to lack of performance and worrying about issues surrounding the test.

Lack of Preparation

Lack of preparation can be identified by the following behaviors or situations:

- Not scheduling enough time to study, and therefore cramming the night before the test or exam
- Managing time poorly, to create the sensation that there is not enough time to do everything
- Failing to organize the text information in advance, so that the study material consists of the entire text and not simply the pertinent information
- Poor overall studying habits

Worrying, on the other hand, can be related to both the test taker, or many other factors around him/her that will be affected by the results of the test. These include worrying about:

- Previous performances on similar exams, or exams in general
- How friends and other students are achieving
- The negative consequences that will result from a poor grade or failure

There are three primary elements to test anxiety. Physical components, which involve the same typical bodily reactions as those to acute anxiety (to be discussed below). Emotional factors have to do with fear or panic. Mental or cognitive issues concerning attention spans and memory abilities.

Physical Signals

There are many different symptoms of test anxiety, and these are not limited to mental and emotional strain. Frequently there are a range of physical signals that will let a test taker know that he/she is suffering from test anxiety. These bodily changes can include the following:

- Perspiring
- Sweaty palms
- Wet, trembling hands
- Nausea
- Dry mouth
- A knot in the stomach
- Headache
- Faintness
- Muscle tension
- Aching shoulders, back and neck
- Rapid heart beat
- Feeling too hot/cold

To recognize the sensation of test anxiety, a test-taker should monitor him/herself for the following sensations:

- The physical distress symptoms as listed above
- Emotional sensitivity, expressing emotional feelings such as the need to cry or laugh too much, or a sensation of anger or helplessness
- A decreased ability to think, causing the test-taker to blank out or have racing thoughts that are hard to organize or control.

Though most students will feel some level of anxiety when faced with a test or exam, the majority can cope with that anxiety and maintain it at a manageable level. However, those who cannot are faced with a very real and very serious condition, which can and should be controlled for the immeasurable benefit of this sufferer.

Naturally, these sensations lead to negative results for the testing experience. The most common effects of test anxiety have to do with nervousness and mental blocking.

Nervousness

Nervousness can appear in several different levels:

- The test-taker's difficulty, or even inability to read and understand the questions on the test
- The difficulty or inability to organize thoughts to a coherent form
- The difficulty or inability to recall key words and concepts relating to the testing questions (especially essays)

- The receipt of poor grades on a test, though the test material was well known by the test taker

Conversely, a person may also experience mental blocking, which involves:

- Blanking out on test questions
- Only remembering the correct answers to the questions when the test has already finished.

Fortunately for test anxiety sufferers, beating these feelings, to a large degree, has to do with proper preparation. When a test taker has a feeling of preparedness, then anxiety will be dramatically lessened.

The first step to resolving anxiety issues is to distinguish which of the two types of anxiety are being suffered. If the anxiety is a direct result of a lack of preparation, this should be considered a normal reaction, and the anxiety level (as opposed to the test results) shouldn't be anything to worry about. However, if, when adequately prepared, the test-taker still panics, blanks out, or seems to overreact, this is not a fully rational reaction. While this can be considered normal too, there are many ways to combat and overcome these effects.

Remember that anxiety cannot be entirely eliminated, however, there are ways to minimize it, to make the anxiety easier to manage. Preparation is one of the best ways to minimize test anxiety. Therefore the following techniques are wise in order to best fight off any anxiety that may want to build.

To begin with, try to avoid cramming before a test, whenever it is possible. By trying to memorize an entire term's worth of information in one day, you'll be shocking your system, and not giving yourself a very good chance to absorb the information. This is an easy path to anxiety, so for those who suffer from test anxiety, cramming should not even be considered an option.

Instead of cramming, work throughout the semester to combine all of the material which is presented throughout the semester, and work on it gradually as the course goes by, making sure to master the main concepts first, leaving minor details for a week or so before the test.

To study for the upcoming exam, be sure to pose questions that may be on the examination, to gauge the ability to answer them by integrating the ideas from your texts, notes and lectures, as well as any supplementary readings.

If it is truly impossible to cover all of the information that was covered in that particular term, concentrate on the most important portions, that can be covered very well. Learn these concepts as best as possible, so that when the test comes, a goal can be made to use these concepts as presentations of your knowledge.

In addition to study habits, changes in attitude are critical to beating a struggle with test anxiety. In fact, an improvement of the perspective over the entire test-taking experience can actually help a test taker to enjoy studying and therefore improve the overall experience. Be certain not to overemphasize the significance of the grade - know that the result of the test is neither a reflection of self worth, nor is it a measure of intelligence; one grade will not predict a person's future success.

To improve an overall testing outlook, the following steps should be tried:

1. Keeping in mind that the most reasonable expectation for taking a test is to expect to try to demonstrate as much of what you know as you possibly can.
2. Reminding ourselves that a test is only one test; this is not the only one, and there will be others.
3. The thought of thinking of oneself in an irrational, all-or-nothing term should be avoided at all costs.
4. A reward should be designated for after the test, so there's something to look forward to. Whether it be going to a movie, going out to eat, or simply visiting friends, schedule it in advance, and do it no matter what result is expected on the exam.

Test-takers should also keep in mind that the basics are some of the most important things, even beyond anti-anxiety techniques and studying. Never neglect the basic social, emotional and biological needs, in order to try to absorb information. In order to best achieve, these three factors must be held as just as important as the studying itself.

Study Steps

Remember the following important steps for studying:

1. Maintain healthy nutrition and exercise habits. Continue both your recreational activities and social pass times. These both contribute to your physical and emotional well being.
2. Be certain to get a good amount of sleep, especially the night before the test, because when you're overtired you are not able to perform to the best of your best ability.
3. Keep the studying pace to a moderate level by taking breaks when they are needed, and varying the work whenever possible, to keep the mind fresh instead of getting bored.
4. When enough studying has been done that all the material that can be learned has been learned, and the test taker is prepared for the test, stop studying and do something relaxing such as listening to music, watching a movie, or taking a warm bubble bath.

There are also many other techniques to minimize the uneasiness or apprehension that is experienced along with test anxiety before, during, or even after the examination. In fact, there are a great deal of things that can be done to stop anxiety from interfering with lifestyle and performance. Again, remember that anxiety will not be eliminated entirely, and it shouldn't be. Otherwise that "up" feeling for exams would not exist, and most of us depend on that sensation to perform better than usual. However, this anxiety has to be at a level that is manageable.

Of course, as we have just discussed, being prepared for the exam is half the battle right away. Attending all classes, finding out what knowledge will be expected on the exam, and knowing the exam schedules are easy steps to lowering anxiety. Keeping up with work will remove the need to cram, and efficient study habits will eliminate wasted time. Studying should be done in an ideal location for concentration, so that it is simple to become interested in the material and give it complete attention. A method such as SQ3R (Survey, Question, Read, Recite, Review) is a wonderful key to follow to make sure that the study habits are as effective as possible, especially in the case of learning from a textbook. Flashcards are great techniques for memorization. Learning to take good notes will mean that notes will be full of useful information, so that less sifting will need to be done to seek out what is pertinent for studying. Reviewing notes after class and then again on occasion will keep the information fresh in the mind. From notes that have been taken summary sheets and outlines can be made for simpler reviewing.

A study group can also be a very motivational and helpful place to study, as there will be a sharing of ideas, all of the minds can work together, to make sure that everyone understands, and the studying will be made more interesting because it will be a social occasion.

Basically, though, as long as the test-taker remains organized and self confident, with efficient study habits, less time will need to be spent studying, and higher grades will be achieved.

To become self confident, there are many useful steps. The first of these is "self talk." It has been shown through extensive research, that self-talk for students who suffer from test anxiety, should be well monitored, in order to make sure that it contributes to self confidence as opposed to sinking the student. Frequently the self talk of test-anxious students is negative or self-defeating, thinking that everyone else is smarter and faster, that they always mess up, and that if they don't do well, they'll fail the entire course. It is important to decreasing anxiety that awareness is made of self talk. Try writing any negative self thoughts and then disputing them with a positive statement instead. Begin self-encouragement as though it was a friend speaking. Repeat positive statements to help reprogram the mind to believing in successes instead of failures.

Helpful Techniques

Other extremely helpful techniques include:

- Self-visualization of doing well and reaching goals
- While aiming for an "A" level of understanding, don't try to "overprotect" by setting your expectations lower. This will only convince the mind to stop studying in order to meet the lower expectations.
- Don't make comparisons with the results or habits of other students. These are individual factors, and different things work for different people, causing different results.
- Strive to become an expert in learning what works well, and what can be done in order to improve. Consider collecting this data in a journal.
- Create rewards for after studying instead of doing things before studying that will only turn into avoidance behaviors.
- Make a practice of relaxing - by using methods such as progressive relaxation, self-hypnosis, guided imagery, etc - in order to make relaxation an automatic sensation.

- Work on creating a state of relaxed concentration so that concentrating will take on the focus of the mind, so that none will be wasted on worrying.
- Take good care of the physical self by eating well and getting enough sleep.
- Plan in time for exercise and stick to this plan.

Beyond these techniques, there are other methods to be used before, during and after the test that will help the test-taker perform well in addition to overcoming anxiety.

Before the exam comes the academic preparation. This involves establishing a study schedule and beginning at least one week before the actual date of the test. By doing this, the anxiety of not having enough time to study for the test will be automatically eliminated. Moreover, this will make the studying a much more effective experience, ensuring that the learning will be an easier process. This relieves much undue pressure on the test-taker.

Summary sheets, note cards, and flash cards with the main concepts and examples of these main concepts should be prepared in advance of the actual studying time. A topic should never be eliminated from this process. By omitting a topic because it isn't expected to be on the test is only setting up the test-taker for anxiety should it actually appear on the exam. Utilize the course syllabus for laying out the topics that should be studied. Carefully go over the notes that were made in class, paying special attention to any of the issues that the professor took special care to emphasize while lecturing in class. In the textbooks, use the chapter review, or if possible, the chapter tests, to begin your review.

It may even be possible to ask the instructor what information will be covered on the exam, or what the format of the exam will be (for example, multiple choice, essay, free form, true-false). Additionally, see if it is possible to find out how many questions will be on the test. If a review sheet or sample test has been offered by the professor, make good use of it, above anything else, for the preparation for the test. Another great resource for getting to know the examination is reviewing tests from previous semesters. Use these tests to review, and aim to achieve a 100% score on each of the possible topics. With a few exceptions, the goal that you set for yourself is the highest one that you will reach.

Take all of the questions that were assigned as homework, and rework them to any other possible course material. The more problems reworked, the more skill and confidence will form as a result. When forming the solution to a problem, write out each of the steps. Don't simply do head work. By doing as many steps on paper as possible, much clarification and therefore confidence will be formed. Do this with as many homework problems as possible, before checking the answers. By checking the answer after each problem, a reinforcement will exist, that will not be on the exam. Study situations should be as exam-like as possible, to prime the test-taker's system for the experience. By waiting to check the answers at the end, a psychological advantage will be formed, to decrease the stress factor.

Another fantastic reason for not cramming is the avoidance of confusion in concepts, especially when it comes to mathematics. 8-10 hours of study will become one hundred percent more effective if it is spread out over a week or at least several days, instead of doing it all in one sitting. Recognize that the human brain requires time in order to assimilate new material, so frequent breaks and a span of study time over several days will be much more beneficial.

Additionally, don't study right up until the point of the exam. Studying should stop a minimum of one hour before the exam begins. This allows the brain to rest and put things in their proper order. This will also provide the time to become as relaxed as possible when going into the examination room. The test-taker will also have time to eat well and eat sensibly. Know that the brain needs food as much as the rest of the body. With enough food and enough sleep, as well as a relaxed attitude, the body and the mind are primed for success.

Avoid any anxious classmates who are talking about the exam. These students only spread anxiety, and are not worth sharing the anxious sentimentalities.

Before the test also involves creating a positive attitude, so mental preparation should also be a point of concentration. There are many keys to creating a positive attitude. Should fears become rushing in, make a visualization of taking the exam, doing well, and seeing an A written on the paper. Write out a list of affirmations that will bring a feeling of confidence, such as "I am doing well in my English class," "I studied well and know my material," "I enjoy this class." Even if the affirmations aren't believed at first, it sends a positive message to the subconscious which will result in an alteration of the overall belief system, which is the system that creates reality.

If a sensation of panic begins, work with the fear and imagine the very worst! Work through the entire scenario of not passing the test, failing the entire course, and dropping out of school, followed by not getting a job, and pushing a shopping cart through the dark alley where you'll live. This will place things into perspective! Then, practice deep breathing and create a visualization of the opposite situation - achieving an "A" on the exam, passing the entire course, receiving the degree at a graduation ceremony.

On the day of the test, there are many things to be done to ensure the best results, as well as the most calm outlook. The following stages are suggested in order to maximize test-taking potential:

1. Begin the examination day with a moderate breakfast, and avoid any coffee or beverages with caffeine if the test taker is prone to jitters. Even people who are used to managing caffeine can feel jittery or light-headed when it is taken on a test day.
2. Attempt to do something that is relaxing before the examination begins. As last minute cramming clouds the mastering of overall concepts, it is better to use this time to create a calming outlook.
3. Be certain to arrive at the test location well in advance, in order to provide time to select a location that is away from doors, windows and other distractions, as well as giving enough time to relax before the test begins.
4. Keep away from anxiety generating classmates who will upset the sensation of stability and relaxation that is being attempted before the exam.
5. Should the waiting period before the exam begins cause anxiety, create a self-distraction by reading a light magazine or something else that is relaxing and simple.

During the exam itself, read the entire exam from beginning to end, and find out how much time should be allotted to each individual problem. Once writing the exam, should more time be taken for a problem, it should be abandoned, in order to begin another problem. If there is time at the end, the unfinished problem can always be returned to and completed.

Read the instructions very carefully - twice - so that unpleasant surprises won't follow during or after the exam has ended.

When writing the exam, pretend that the situation is actually simply the completion of homework within a library, or at home. This will assist in forming a relaxed atmosphere, and will allow the brain extra focus for the complex thinking function.

Begin the exam with all of the questions with which the most confidence is felt. This will build the confidence level regarding the entire exam and will begin a quality momentum. This will also create encouragement for trying the problems where uncertainty resides.

Going with the "gut instinct" is always the way to go when solving a problem. Second guessing should be avoided at all costs. Have confidence in the ability to do well.

For essay questions, create an outline in advance that will keep the mind organized and make certain that all of the points are remembered. For multiple choice, read every answer, even if the correct one has been spotted - a better one may exist.

Continue at a pace that is reasonable and not rushed, in order to be able to work carefully. Provide enough time to go over the answers at the end, to check for small errors that can be corrected.

Should a feeling of panic begin, breathe deeply, and think of the feeling of the body releasing sand through its pores. Visualize a calm, peaceful place, and include all of the sights, sounds and sensations of this image. Continue the deep breathing, and take a few minutes to continue this with closed eyes. When all is well again, return to the test.

If a "blanking" occurs for a certain question, skip it and move on to the next question. There will be time to return to the other question later. Get everything done that can be done, first, to guarantee all the grades that can be compiled, and to build all of the confidence possible. Then return to the weaker questions to build the marks from there.

Remember, one's own reality can be created, so as long as the belief is there, success will follow. And remember: anxiety can happen later, right now, there's an exam to be written!

After the examination is complete, whether there is a feeling for a good grade or a bad grade, don't dwell on the exam, and be certain to follow through on the reward that was promised...and enjoy it! Don't dwell on any mistakes that have been made, as there is nothing that can be done at this point anyway.

Additionally, don't begin to study for the next test right away. Do something relaxing for a while, and let the mind relax and prepare itself to begin absorbing information again. From the results of the exam - both the grade and the entire experience, be certain to learn from what has gone on. Perfect studying habits and work some more on confidence in order to make the next examination experience even better than the last one.

Learn to avoid places where openings occurred for laziness, procrastination and day dreaming.

Use the time between this exam and the next one to better learn to relax, even learning to relax on cue, so that any anxiety can be controlled during the next exam. Learn how to relax the body. Slouch in your chair if that helps. Tighten and then relax all of the different muscle groups, one group at a time, beginning with the feet and then working all the way up to the neck and face. This will ultimately relax the muscles more than they were to begin with. Learn how to breathe deeply and comfortably, and focus on this breathing going in and out as a relaxing thought. With every exhale, repeat the word "relax."

As common as test anxiety is, it is very possible to overcome it. Make yourself one of the test-takers who overcome this frustrating hindrance.

Special Report: Retaking the Test: What Are Your Chances at Improving Your Score?

After going through the experience of taking a major test, many test takers feel that once is enough. The test usually comes during a period of transition in the test taker's life, and taking the test is only one of a series of important events. With so many distractions and conflicting recommendations, it may be difficult for a test taker to rationally determine whether or not he should retake the test after viewing his scores.

The importance of the test usually only adds to the burden of the retake decision. However, don't be swayed by emotion. There a few simple questions that you can ask yourself to guide you as you try to determine whether a retake would improve your score:

1. What went wrong? Why wasn't your score what you expected?

Can you point to a single factor or problem that you feel caused the low score? Were you sick on test day? Was there an emotional upheaval in your life that caused a distraction? Were you late for the test or not able to use the full time allotment? If you can point to any of these specific, individual problems, then a retake should definitely be considered.

2. Is there enough time to improve?

Many problems that may show up in your score report may take a lot of time for improvement. A deficiency in a particular math skill may require weeks or months of tutoring and studying to improve. If you have enough time to improve an identified weakness, then a retake should definitely be considered.

3. How will additional scores be used? Will a score average, highest score, or most recent score be used?

Different test scores may be handled completely differently. If you've taken the test multiple times, sometimes your highest score is used, sometimes your average score is computed and used, and sometimes your most recent score is used. Make sure you understand what method will be used to evaluate your scores, and use that to help you determine whether a retake should be considered.

4. Are my practice test scores significantly higher than my actual test score?

If you have taken a lot of practice tests and are consistently scoring at a much higher level than your actual test score, then you should consider a retake. However, if you've taken five practice tests and only one of your scores was higher than your actual test score, or if your practice test scores were only slightly higher than your actual test score, then it is unlikely that you will significantly increase your score.

5. Do I need perfect scores or will I be able to live with this score? Will this score still allow me to follow my dreams?

What kind of score is acceptable to you? Is your current score "good enough?" Do you have to have a certain score in order to pursue the future of your dreams? If you won't be happy with your current score, and there's no way that you could live with it, then you should consider a retake. However, don't get your hopes up. If you are looking for significant improvement, that may or may not be possible. But if you won't be happy otherwise, it is at least worth the effort.

Remember that there are other considerations. To achieve your dream, it is likely that your grades may also be taken into account. A great test score is usually not the only thing necessary to succeed. Make sure that you aren't overemphasizing the importance of a high test score.

Furthermore, a retake does not always result in a higher score. Some test takers will score lower on a retake, rather than higher. One study shows that one-fourth of test takers will achieve a significant improvement in test score, while one-sixth of test takers will actually show a decrease. While this shows that most test takers will improve, the majority will only improve their scores a little and a retake may not be worth the test taker's effort.

Finally, if a test is taken only once and is considered in the added context of good grades on the part of a test taker, the person reviewing the grades and scores may be tempted to assume that the test taker just had a bad day while taking the test, and may discount the low test score in favor of the high grades. But if the test is retaken and the scores are approximately the same, then the validity of the low scores are only confirmed. Therefore, a retake could actually hurt a test taker by definitely bracketing a test taker's score ability to a limited range.

Special Report: Additional Bonus Material

Due to our efforts to try to keep this book to a manageable length, we've created a link that will give you access to all of your additional bonus material.

Please visit http://www.mometrix.com/bonus948/nystcescbuildl to access the information.